VOGUE
MODERN STYLE

Charlotte Du Cann was born in London in
1956. She spent two years at *Vogue* and has
subsequently worked as a writer and stylist
for various magazines, including *Tatler*,
Harpers & Queen, *The World of Interiors* and
Elle. This is her first book on fashion.

CHARLOTTE DU CANN

VOGUE
MODERN STYLE

CENTURY
LONDON MELBOURNE AUCKLAND JOHANNESBURG

Copyright © Charlotte Du Cann 1988

Photographs © The Condé Nast Publications Ltd

All rights reserved

First published in 1988 by Century Hutchinson Ltd,
Brookmount House, 62–65 Chandos Place, Covent Garden,
London WC2N 4NW

Century Hutchinson Australia Pty Ltd, PO Box 496,
16–22 Church Street, Hawthorn, Victoria 3122, Australia

Century Hutchinson New Zealand Limited, PO Box 40–086,
Glenfield, Auckland 10, New Zealand

Century Hutchinson South Africa (Pty) Ltd, PO Box 337,
Bergvlei 2012, South Africa

Designed by Paul Bowden
Picture research Jane Ross

Set in Garamond and Helvetica

Printed and bound in Great Britain by
Butler and Tanner Ltd, Frome

British Library Cataloguing in Publication Data
Du Cann, Charlotte, *1956* –
Vogue – modern style:
how to achieve it.
1. Fashion
I. Title
746.9′2

ISBN 0 7126 1802 3 (cased)
0 7126 1807 4 (paper)

Cover photograph: *Modern style evening dress in black
silk taffeta by Oscar de la Renta*
Frontispiece: *Top knotch by Didier Malige for Jean
Louis David*

CONTENTS

For Danny

INTRODUCTION

FASHION. Once this meant the rule of the hemline, the reign of Balenciaga and the power that was Paris. Fashion dictated, the world obeyed.

Fashion then went cap in hand with the rest of society, you knew your place and you dressed accordingly. By the eighties these formal attitudes had shifted. The consumer age said, Look at this! Do you want it? Have it! All things became instantly purchasable, dream homes, dream holidays, dream frocks. Just sign on the dotted line.

Fashion became style. Where there had been home editors there became style editors, where there had been DIY decorating there were style books. Instead of living according to your means, you had a life-style. For the first time there were alternative ways of dressing and designing that didn't demand a socio-political statement, that didn't mean being seen as an outsider or a recluse or, at best, artistic.

Some of this style sprang from the anarchic narrative of the so-called street fashion that declared 'You can be who you want' with outrageous confidence. As these different looks streamed out of changing clubs and were charted by the style journalists, they began to influence the way everyone dressed. The pavement climbed on to the catwalk. And the looks, from Vivienne Westwood's Hobo Look to Katherine Hamnett's Hippy Look, coincided perfectly with the new marketing that everyone saw on their screens and in the magazines. In 1984 when the original book *More Dash Than Cash* (of which this is the sequel) was published, style was only just pushing into the mainstream. The emphasis of that book was still on pure fashion, it was still on how to dress like the grown-ups without spending so much money. This was before the world of hype fed by pictures, before Next, *Frocks on the Box*, the notion of powerdressing and designer desirables. In 1988 in the age of style, it is no longer possible to write such a book. People's perceptions have changed irrevocably.

CHECKMATE!
Opposite, *Jasper Conran's houndstooth suit worn with grey felt trilby by Stephen Jones*

IN THE BLACK
Above, *Black velvet ankle-length coat and jodhpurs from Harvey Nichols with curly brimmed top hat from Hackett*

HEADSTRONG
Opposite, *Straw hat with yellow and violet flowers by Cavalli and Nastri*

ON YER BIKE
Right, *Jean Paul Gaultier's black cotton redingote over white cotton camisole and skirt*

Modern Style grew from a desire to create a book that would group all the classic 'looks' together, all the key styles in a witty reference book. Though the emphasis on the word style has implied individuality, in reality it means choice. Not one style for each person but several styles for everybody. *Modern Style* charts this choice from the city to the country, from Japan to Milan, styles influenced by period nostalgia, films, certain people, other places. It lists the elements that make the essential modern wardrobe – a redirected attitude to keeping clothes,

now that fashion no longer dies each season. *Modern Style* is also about narrative British style and the Modern Girl.

British style loves to tell a story. Stories from the past, stories from abroad. The modern girl weaves a story into everything she wears: a shawl from a grandmother's trunk, a belt from the bazaar at Marrakesh, a tweed jacket from a country house. Like a magpie, Modern Girl will plunder history to fit a moment. She will mix old with new, a designer label with a chain-store tag, she dresses to amuse herself and to suit the circumstance.

This liberty to dress according to your pleasure, not according to status and price tag, is a British quality that does not exist in other countries, yet it is widely copied. Modern Girl, though cosmopolitan, has no love for the blandness of internationalism nor for peer uniforms (i.e. executive or powerdressing). She likes to be noticed but she doesn't dress to impress. British Style, Modern Style is a democracy not a dictatorship.

Nor is it a costume ball. In the mid-eighties style became confused with the idea of dressing up. *Modern Style*, working from a permanent collection of basics (from the black polo neck to the essential pair of shades) and classics, uses 'looks' and outside influences for an extension of the visual self, not as a cover up. *Modern Style* is about living in the real world not at a carnival ball. Modern Girl knows the fine line between fun and fantasy, knows the difference between you wearing the clothes and the clothes wearing you. This is *not* a book for fashion victims. In 1988 the key word is confidence. There are no chapters on What Length Hem or Can You Take a Picture Hat because *Modern Style* assumes a certain modern assurance. The assurance of knowing what you want and finding out how to achieve it. Be bold.

BLOOMING CHIC
Top, *Black baggy bloomers and hooded top in cotton jersey from Harvey Nichols*

TRUE BLUE
Left, *Blue and white striped cardigan by Giorgio Grati and navy blue pleated mini skirt by Costume National*

SECOND SKIN
Opposite, *A zipped black velvet dress by Complice*

CLASSICS

What is a classic? Neither old nor new, it is the timeless and universal fashion that never lets you down. The fashion that appears on each season's catwalk from the Little Black Dress to the Trench. Though there may be subtle shifts of emphasis, a change of collar, colour or length of hem, the classic endures in spirit.

Classic dressing is about confidence. The classic doesn't pretend to be anything else, it doesn't play games, with time or place or gender, it doesn't yearn for sudden bursts of wit or fashion detail. It wouldn't dream of making a scene which is why the classic, at the risk of appearing dull, is acceptable everywhere and never ends up in the dressing-up box.

Classic dressing is never messy and takes its modern style from the cool immaculate women of film: Grace Kelly, Lauren Bacall, Katharine Hepburn. It requires a sober sense of self-restraint and calm, particularly when buying, for the classic aspires always to superior cut and quality of cloth for which there are few substitutes. So though classic dressing may cost more than other styles, the clothes last longer.

The key classic word is *investment*.

Opposite, *Katharine Hepburn*;
inset top, *Katharine Hepburn
and Spencer Tracy*; inset below,
Veronica Lake
This page, top to bottom,
*Audrey Hepburn, Grace Kelly,
Lauren Bacall*

17

SWEATER DRESSING

Sweaterdressing is one step beyond executive, a working style without the hard edges of the tailored suit. It is both strict and casual at the same time, a wolf in sheep's clothing. And, in the best classical tradition, it is both timeless and international (the exception being Milan where the sweaters show off horribly, throwing wild animal appliqué or lurex over the shoulder pads and misbehave generally). Sweaterdressing is best exemplified by the American citystyle, a no-fuss, no-frills puritan ethic that was captured so brilliantly by Calvin Klein.

Sweaterdressing has to be plain, plain, plain whatever the style, worn with the plainest pants, serious skirts, straightforward accessories. The colours are muted and unobtrusive: metropolitan monochrome, power-house beige, neutrals or deep sombres such as burgundy. There are no brights here and certainly no creative clash. The wool must be wool or the best imitation, lambswool preferably and cashmere if you can afford it. The secret is to keep the weave fine, then even cotton will do. Anything loosely acrylic won't. There are no rugged textures for the sweatergirl, who never takes her wools outside, let alone outside the city (for the rough stuff, see the Weather Dressing chapter).

THE TWINSET

The Twinset, once reviled as the epitome of Supersloane style, has now established itself as an ironic classic. When Katherine Hamnett made twinsets in white cotton in 1986 and the Japanese began to cut their cloth more sweetly to produce the essential cropped cardigan in *eau de nil*, everybody remembered how *fabulous* Grace Kelly looked in one.

Twinset cheat 1: if you can't afford designer, some chainstores still produce twinsets for granny with pearls. If the buttons are boring *snip them off*, and replace with silver or jet.

Twinset cheat 2: put a short cardigan with a T-shirt of the same colour. No sweatergirl wants to be the heroine in *Hotel du Lac* in a droopy, depressing cardigan *à la* Virginia Woolf.

Twinset colours: pale, i.e., cream or shell pink, or strong black *à la* Chanel.

THE POLO NECK

The Polo Neck is the sweater of hip. What beatpoet or jazzman would have been seen without one? It's the sax in the wardrobe, a mean, ubiquitous jersey. No one ever looked uncool in one. Apart from bohemian black, there is the Breton striped polo (for French nautical style), the white European polo worn underneath a heavier sweater or with a suit (think Dirk Bogarde, see Sixties, Retro) and there is the American richwool turtleneck which practically *has* to be in cream.

Polo note: the polo can be bought anywhere these days, designer store to chainstore. Men's stores and skiing departments are best for cotton in every colour. The bad news with the polo is always in the neck. Cheap ones stretch and sag. Clever pinning with a brooch is a solution but a far better thing to do is *chuck it out* (and buy another).

THE SWEATERDRESS

The Sweaterdress, like the coatdress, is an acquired taste. Not every sweatergirl leaps for the woolly frock in the morning. The Sweaterdress can be unkind to curves but can look fabulous with fabulous legs (which should always be in opaque tights, cotton preferably, with a flat, simple shoe). It is not to be confused with the long jumper often worn with leggings which is a way too casual sportif look for the sweatergirl who is cool and collected at all times.

Sweaterdress Details: always belted, the Sweaterdress loves thick, wrapped suede or metal chain *à la* Chanel (never anything thin, aggressive or studded), metal bangles or large watch worn over sleeve.

Sweaterdress Colours: more cream, chocolate brown, taupe, slate or olive.

Woolnotes

Sweatergirl *never*:
– slings a sweater about her shoulders or ties it around her waist.
– layers or knots her wool in interesting ways. She favours English rose over Japanese black.
– wears anything underneath her wool (no collars peeping out).

THE CAST OF CHARACTERS

Opposite, *Pure and simple Shetland polo-dress with strategic accessories*
Top, *Cream cotton turtleneck teamed up with baggy linen pants*
Above, *Matching lambswool sweater and skirt pulled together with a cunning chain belt*

THE GREAT WHITE SHIRT

What other fashion item could be quite as versatile as the Great White Shirt? Why, it can practically never go wrong. It fits underneath for winter, stays cool for summer, can be formal, informal or dramatically flamboyant (what would Errol or Romeo or Byron have done without their white shirts?). It can be governessy starchy and prim, it can be wickedly transparent. It is the stuff of school uniforms and parades, of offices, functions and fieldwork.

This shirt likes to appear in every corner. Essential wardrobe likes at least six.

The Classic Collar: stiff Eton collar, soft collar, wing collar, wrap collar, no collar (but never a Peter Pan or a lace fringed collar).

Honorary White Shirt: blue and white pinstripe borrowed from the boys.

Formal White: piqué dress shirt, also borrowed from the boys (leave the bow tie out).

Ethnic White: long Indian muslin (*not* cheesecloth), Nehru, Tibetan, Chinese mandarin collar.

White Shirt Alternative: white pyjama tops.

GREAT WHITE CLASSICS

Left, *The Flirtshirt in white silk organza by Calvin Klein*
Below left, *The long-sleeved Puritan in white cotton by Romeo Gigli*
Below right, *The short-sleeved Soft Collar in white cotton from Flip*

WORKSHIRT

The Workshirt is very plain. The plainest item you own. It's so bland you practically don't notice its presence. The Workshirt is fine cotton (doesn't tolerate artificial fibres even though it would make ironing irrelevant). It likes all its buttons done up, including those at the end of its perfectly starched arms. The Workshirt would love a tie but you don't let it have one. You might shock it with a frivolous twist of coloured scarf, or a piece of diamanté to soften its glare. For the Workshirt must glow, if it doesn't it must go.

For white to be grey is as bad as Being Late For Work.

ROUGHSHIRT

The Roughshirt is a workaday outdoor cotton. Has to be. It comes in two forms, the short-sleeved safari and the long-sleeved Puritan.

The short-sleeved Roughshirt belongs to the outback and the African veldt, sometimes sporting a short tie. Beloved of Chanel who teamed it perfectly with jodhpurs. It also looks great with pressed baggy shorts and khaki or sailor white trousers. The short sleeve is about as relaxed a classic as you can get but maybe that is the heat.

Roughshirt 2 is the larger cut Workshirt, with a soft or no collar, and owes its spirit to the preacher style of the MidWest. It is about as sober a classic as you can get (no frills or fashion details for this white).

Roughshirt note: both forms spring up in every chainstore every season. Alternatives abound in second-hand stores and markets. Although it has to be said, as with the rest of the sections, to find the perfect Great White Shirt is the hardest task of them all.

FLIRTSHIRT

The Flirtshirt is the white that loves the night and likes its buttons undone. The Flirtshirt, unlike its cousins, doesn't hide the body but flaunts it. Soft collared, shawl collared, it can be transparent, it can roll its sleeves up, it can even be daringly cream. Most of all it likes to be in silk.

Silkdressing is a chameleon art, for it can transform a pair of jeans into a classic style and it can be relied upon to soften any executive line. Silkdressing loves plain dark colours, especially black and navy.

Modern Silk: the modern classic silk shirt was practically invented by Katherine Hamnett. Generously cut in crumpled parachute silk, it has appeared in every hue from jewelled purple to soft apricot. But best, of course, in white.

LIGHT CLASSICS
by Margaret Howell
Above, *The pique bibbed cotton dress shirt*
Right, *The short-sleeved cotton rough shirt*

24

**THE CLASSIC
PANTS**
Right, *Biscuit linen twill
turn-ups by Calvin Klein*
Opposite page, *White
linen turn-ups by
Aquascutum*

CLASSIC PANTS

The absolute point of the pant classical is the tailoring. Those slacks have got to be beautifully cut in good fabric – cotton and linen in summer, flannel, tweed or wool for winter. The Classic Pant must never be flirty, tight, cropped or be anything approaching a legging. It can be pleated or bagged, have turnups or buttons but it must have strength. The Classic Pant is the epitome of casual power. No one would wear the Classic Pant without knowing *exactly* who they were.

The wearer always has the last word (think of Bette Davis) and has no need of steely skirts or shoulder pads as cursory nods towards femininity.

The Classic Pant looks great with real simplicity: plain flat shoes (never heels), pumps, brogues, even plimsolls. It loves a plain round neck or polo neck sweater or straightforward shirt.

The Americans are best at wearing the Classic Pant where the tradition is relentlessly updated by Ralph Lauren. Often found in a suit and worn separately, the Classic Pant loves the forties (see Retro) and hates shorties.

Classic Pant Detail: The Belt. Never too rich and never too thin for the classical belt. Very particular about its quiet leather and croc. Particularly loathes patent leather or anything that doesn't go into the hoops.

Classic Pant Colours (winter): navy, black, chocolate, Prince of Wales check, grey.

(summer): navy, white, sand.

Modern Classic: the modern Classic Pant is the 501 Levi jean. No other textile, no other shape has cornered the globe as successfully as these two blue legs. It is the Coca Cola of the fashion industry. Classical jeans are neither ripped nor ironed but worn in the same spirit as the classic pants.

TURN UP FOR THE LOOK
Below, *Narrow taupe cotton turn-ups by Katherine Hamnett* Right, *Baggy white cotton men's trousers from Hackett*

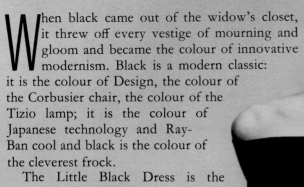

When black came out of the widow's closet, it threw off every vestige of mourning and gloom and became the colour of innovative modernism. Black is a modern classic: it is the colour of Design, the colour of the Corbusier chair, the colour of the Tizio lamp; it is the colour of Japanese technology and Ray-Ban cool and black is the colour of the cleverest frock.

The Little Black Dress is the epitome of gamine chic. If black has connotations of seriousness and masculine imagination, then the LBD is quite the opposite: the LBD is a wicked flirt. It can play at being prim with long sleeves and ballerina skirt or schoolgirl sweet with a dropwaist but mostly it is itself, witty and sophisticated. It can be soft in velvet, strictly tailored in wool, it can be in rayon or raw silk, clinging tightly or standing out in an A-line. The LBD can be loaded with accessories, *faux* pearls and chains, heavy bracelets, long drop earrings (but nothing gimmicky or ethnic). It disdains watches or belts but looks brilliant with dramatic hats, long gloves, handbags and high hair (think of Audrey Hepburn in *Breakfast at Tiffany's*). However, the LBD itself must be plain, must be short – a sleek shape that glides effortlessly through the day into cocktail hour. What wardrobe would be complete without one?

THE LITTLE BLACK DRESS

BODY-CONSCIOUS BLACK

Left, *Norma Kamali's racy jersey dress with cut-away neckline, and snappy handbag* Middle, *Jasper Conran's strapless velvet sheath dress, and sculptural silver* Opposite page, *Versace's short ruched jersey dress, and tall felt hat*

CLASSIC COVER-UPS
Opposite above, *Herringbone tweed by Margaret Howell*
Opposite below, *Double-breasted camel with leather buttons and buckles by Aquascutum*
Right, *Wrap in chocolate brown gabardine by Azzedine Alaia*

CLASSIC COATS

Now the Classic Coat is the show-off of winter and it learnt its great swagger from the boys. If you think of Diaghilev's astrakhan-collared full-length, Cecil Beaton in his arrogant cape, Humphrey Bogart in that trench underneath the streetlamp, then you can understand the romance and cool of the Classic Coat.

This coat has to have authority and weight: it is not some sweet girlish schoolcoat or something amusing in PVC. It is not a greatcoat that has staggered out of some old war, and it is not a jacket of any description. It is long, it is strong and it likes its wool heavy (cotton is for duster coat, see Weather Dressing).

Coatnote: the Classic Coat changes with country. In some parts of Europe, the fur coat is worn almost as a uniform, as is the dull-green loden coat (especially in Italy and Austria). Classic Coat, modern style, never looks like a uniform, it may be similar in shape but there are always nuances of difference.

THE CAMEL

The Camel is the toffee-coloured classic, the sleek ponytail of the closet. It can come belted, buckled or cut like a kimono, fitted, waisted or cropped short like a car coat. Whatever shape, it must be the right size and it mustn't look mean.

The Camel lives quite happily in town and country which accounts for its great popularity. Whether dressed in jeans or perfectly cut pants, the Camel guarantees The Rich Casual Look (which is why it draws the line at gumboots). The Camel, ubiquitous coat, is impervious to age. You can never be too old or too bold to wear it.

Thrift Note: like the classic pants, the temptation to buy second-hand men's versions of the Camel is great. There are many fine Camels in many fine thrift stores. But a true classic does not want to look like Orson Welles. You cannot disappear into any classic, you have to look as if you own it rather than it owns you.

Scarf Note: the Camel is fond of scarves. Pale coloured wool or cashmere scarves tied nonchalantly. It also favours gloves of leather or wool (*not* mittens).

THE CAPE

The Cape is one of those classics that appeals to a select few. You have to walk tall to get away with a Cape, whether in opera black or raincoat biscuit. The Cape is not a cloak, it never sports a hood (classical girl does not wish to remind anyone of piety). It always appears as though it has just been thrown on with all the grand gesture of a Veronese painting.

Remember the Big Sweep? The Big Sweep was the big news of the early eighties when Calvin Klein was king of the seams. But its legacy lives. The alternative Cape is the sweep of good material, from a length of ethnic fabric to a generously made wool scarf. Avoid *at all costs* looking like Eliza Doolittle.

CLASSIC OVERTONES
Above, *Trench in biscuit linen by Ralph Lauren*
Opposite, *Mackintosh in beige cotton poplin by Paul Smith*

THE MAC

The Classic Mac is not to be confused with a raincoat. The Classic Mac, like the panama, can be worn in all weathers. It is a very distant cousin of the windcheater and bears no relation to the anorak. The mac never forgets that it is a coat, not something you crumple into a ball, just in case of showers.

Classic Mac takes its shape in two cuts: the riding mac, a single-buttoned collared short knee-length, or the double-breasted belted trench worn formally. Both these shapes can be bought at huge expense at traditional places such as Burberrys but clever mac takes the option.

Mac Options: School macs, riding macs, second-hand men's macs, policemen's mac from NYC, Drizabone sheepshearers' macs from the outback (but *never* a Barbour).

Mac Colours: all varieties of the pale brown – fawn, beige, stone, cream, olive, school slate, school navy.

Umbrella Notes: if it does rain, of course, the macpack take their umbrella plain, severe black, wooden handle (nothing in the shape of ducks). The classic umbrella does not shoot into shape, be pink and/or jolly or have transparent windows or shoulder straps. If there is no umbrella the macpack like a hat. Especially when wearing a trench, especially a trilby *à la* Lauren Bacall. They do not possess gumboots.

CHINESE TAKEAWAY
Lemon linen cropped jacket and
scarlet linen bag turn-ups from
Focus and straw cartwheel hat from
The Hat Shop

ANOTHER

If travel broadens the mind, then it certainly fills up the wardrobe. Modern Girl gets wildly inspired by other countries' dress and scours the foreign markets like a magpie. Designers through the decades have acted similarly, borrowing shamelessly from other nations (YSL's Spanish Look to Jean Paul Gaultier's Russian Constructivist collection to Romeo Gigli's new nomads) as manufacturers have rifled through the empires for rare and beautiful textiles (Chinese silk to Egyptian cotton to African prints).

Within every culture there is a national style that has been translated wittily into an international one: the working dungarees of the Deep South farmer became a global adoption of faded blue denim; the ancient arts of wrapping kimonos and sarongs by the East led to clever twistings of cloth by the West.

However, Modern Girl is wary of the costume ball syndrome. Lawrence of Arabia might have got away with walking down Piccadilly in full-flowing Arab robes but nobody else will. And whereas baggy flowerprint trousers might have been fine while browsing along the Turkish coast they will not necessarily look quite so splendid winging through the supermarket.

Now voyager steers clear of excessive statement at all times but never comes back from vacation with an empty suitcase.

COUNTRY

FRENCH DRESSING Opposite, *Le Beat Look – a black beret worn with black wool coat, trousers and polo neck all by Rifat Ozbek* This page, *The sharp city suit – left, in grey, green and blue plaid by Jasmine,* right, *in Prince of Wales check by Veronica*

BOULEVARD CHIC

C*'est quoi Paris?* What is that style that strides the cobbled street and sits so pertly on a café chair? *C'est chic, chérie.* There is no other word and no other city has it. That elegant *froideur,* that certain love of witty tailoring, that unmistakable confidence and passionate eye for detail.

Boulevard Chic is the woman in the hat that sits perched at an *amusant* angle. She wears a crisp little suit and polished shoes. Her perfect legs are crossed. She never has a *problème* catching the waiter's eye.

Boulevard Chic is the girl crossing the square with matelot stripes and beatnik black stove pipes and a tousled tomboy haircut. Her lips are red, her shoes are flat. That's gamine, that's confidence, that's Paris.

If you want to get there, put these key items in your suitcase:

PRINCE OF WALES

The Prince of Wales check is the tartan of the boulevard. BC likes it in classic pants with turnups and thin belt worn with a black polo neck jersey. BC likes it as the short skirt worn *à la* Chanel with soft white shirt and lots of gold chain. BC likes it as a tailored suit with roomy trousers and a trilby.

LEGS

Fab legs are intrinsic to this city of couture. BC shows them off at any opportunity. Sheer stockings, black high heels, very short skirts worn with long clever jackets, preferably by J P G. BC would never show a leg that had been anywhere near a gym. *Mince* is the word.

THE LITTLE SUIT

The little suit was created, like many great 20th-century concepts, by the *grande dame* of Paris, Coco Chanel. The wool bouclé two piece with straight skirt and collarless jacket is a BC classic, loaded or not with costume jewellery.

THE BERET

The hat of France is not restricted to cartoon onion sellers. BC wears her beret in the spirit of Juliet Greco with a good deal of bohemian black. Very existentialist, very left bank, very BC.

SPRING

If Rome style, *dolce vita* style is summer, then Paris is definitely spring. BC has no truck with heavy coats or knits. Leave them behind. Take a (well cut) jacket or short biscuit trench.

COLOURS

Gitane blue, French navy, black and cream.

CITY SLICKERS

Below left, *Givenchy gamine in white collared and cuffed grey linen suit with wide-brimmed straw hat* Below right, *Business Chic in houndstooth suit by Jasper Conran and grey felt trilby by Stephen Jones* Opposite, *Working girls in* (left) *grey wool flannel suit by Premonville and Dewarin;* (right) *black-and-white kilt balloon skirt by Jean Paul Gaultier*

SPANISH STYLE

AH MI CORRIDA
Top, *A black high-waisted skirt, wide sash and white cotton shirt – all by Saint Laurent Rive Gauche. Broad-brimmed matador hat by Sandra Phillips.*
Above, *Cotton bolero by Ernestina Cerini, high-waisted pants by Romeo Gigli and top by Martine Sitbon*
Opposite, *PRIMA DOÑA: Catherine Bailey by David Bailey*

Spanish Style is a hot Latin mix of Brazilian dancer, Madrid matador and Mexican movie extra. It throws bullfighting capes, flamenco skirts and Navajo silver jewellery together and wears it as haughtily as you please.

The most famous Spanish Style comes from the bullring and *corrida*, the stark dramatics borrowed from the picadors and the Spanish riding masters (the matador's Suit of Lights is a little overmuch even for the supreme show-off style in Europe). The colours are brilliant white and black with scarlet: high-waisted tight trousers, cropped jackets or boleros, cummerbunds and extravagant white shirts. The black riding jackets have silver buttons and the hat is flat and severe. You need to have the straightest back and the palest skin to get away with this one.

Fiesta is the wild side of South America: virulent colour (parrot green, mango, lime), whirling, rippling carnival skirts and low scoopneck blouses or black leotards. Fiesta is a dance style: it loves to tango in red, cha cha in white, while the men wear their chinos rolled and their straw hats distressed.

Spanish Films: *Blood Wedding, Death in the Afternoon, Cuba.*
Spanish Details: white skin, character shoes, black lace, fringed shawls, hooped earrings (but don't overdo the gypsy connection, you don't want to be taken for a fortune teller).
Spanish Opera: *Carmen.*
Spanish Omelettes: sombreros, ponchos, gaucho pants.

LA DOLCE VITA

La Dolce Vita is the sweet sidewalk life that happens somewhere
between Rome and Capri. It needs the summer and it needs the
boys on Vespas and it needs that mixture of slum sex siren and
barefoot contessa that can only speak operatic Italian.

La Dolce Vita is the boys in sharp mafia suits and girls in A-line
sundresses, and everyone in shades. It needs bare arms, little gloves,
big beads and flat shoes. Real *Dolce Vita* is late fifties/early sixties. Its
modern equivalent is the Americano panarini style of chinos, Levi
jackets and lumberjack shirts. Do not confuse the two. Signorina only
walks the strada with a man in a white shirt and tie.

CAPRI PANTS

Capri is where *la dolce signorina* takes her vacation and she wears its high-waisted cropped pants with bravado. The Capri Pant is not to be confused with the matador pant (for a start it doesn't come in black), or the pedal pusher. The Capri always has a side zip, peep-toe heeled sandals, boat neck tops (particularly striped) and a hairdo.

Capri Colours: vivids – scarlet, acid yellow, or ice-cream.

THE ROMAN FROCK

The Roman Frock is the spaghetti version of the Little Black Dress, an outdoor line that can be plain, can be patterned but always worn with sensuality. The Roman Frock loves a halter neck.

Dolce Films: *La Dolce Vita, The Roman Holiday of Mrs Stone.*
Dolce Stars: Marcello Mastroianni, Sophia Loren, Maria Callas.
Dolce Details: shopping baskets, headscarves.
Dolce Designer Star: Pucci.
Dolce Shoe: stiletto.

SPAGHETTI VERSIONS

Opposite, *A strapless cotton print frock by Virginia with mottled beads by Pellini*
Above, *Striding down the strada in black and white striped cotton sweater by Joseph and black jersey capri pants by Claire Dedeyan*

JAPSTYLE

Japstyle is the supreme modern style, the style that yanked fashion from its seventies nostalgia right into the monochrome eighties. The designer samurai swathed through the European traditions and turned their design principles (as well as the clothes themselves) completely upside down. No other country has singlehandedly caused quite so much outrage and adulation in such a short time as Japan.

Japstyle has nothing to do with nostalgia: no wistful longing for white faces, geisha kimonos or cherry blossom. Japstyle is an attitude to cloth that has no bearing on convention. It cuts and wraps without exploiting the body which has led to enthusiasm (freedom at last!) or accusation ('You look like a nuclear bag lady'). The reasons for this are dimly buried in the ancient kimono but the given reasons are about as complicated and minimal as the tea ceremony.

In spite of the Zen stars now becoming more assimilated into European consciousness, Japstyle lives. Its essentials include a sombre palette of neutrals, blacks, inky blues and thunder greys mixed with black and white checks, a feeling for textures, echoing those used in Japanese houses (stone, earth, wood and woven tatami mat) and a play with proportion. If you wear something deliberately oversize it can become instantly Japanese, especially if tucked with pins or held up by braces. The key concepts are asymmetry and non-structure. It's about as far as you can get from the tailored city suit.

MADE IN JAPAN
Opposite, *Matsuda's rough cream cotton shirt and high-backed trousers with a buttoned sling holding the matching pocket blazer*
Right, *Brushed cotton square dress by Lawrence, cotton jersey track trousers by Goldie, sandals and headwrap by Comme des Garçons*

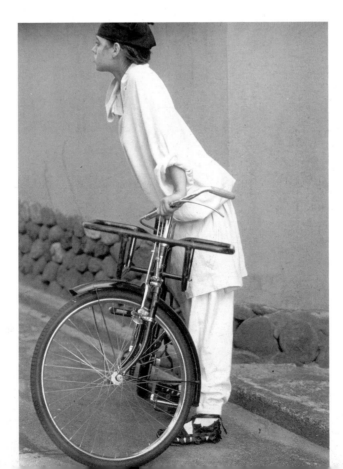

Jap Designer Stars:
Yohji Yamamoto, Issey Miyake, Comme
des Garçons.
Jap Shoes: flat heavy sandals,
wrapped feet.
Jap Fave Fabric: rayon.
Jap Details: headwrap, the huge
white shirt, no collar, gloomy
makeup, wrinkled white stockings.

JAPANTHEON
Opposite, *Bunched black and
white wraps by Yohji
Yamamoto*
Above, *Baggy dark navy
rayon dress by Comme des
Garçons*
Right, *Black parachute
skirt, long white shirt, graffiti
socks and black canvas shoes
by Comme des Garçons*

51

THE COUNTRY GIRLS
Left, *Plain clothes dressing with a blue and white cotton shirt with a man's lambswool cardigan by Pringle* Opposite, *Pioneer women dressed by Nicoletta (left) and Jean Bruno Colomb (right)*

COUNTRY

Country is the romantic notion of the American Midwest from the Amish communities to Nashville, Tennessee. It's a blue collar style of working clothes: tough shirts, overalls, strong knits. It's a kind of Edwardian roughwear mixed with a thirties farmers' make-do (see Retro).

PIONEER WOMAN

Pioneer woman is stern but homely. She wears her Puritan blouse with all the buttons done up and occasionally adorned with cameos and lace collars. Her self-striped long skirts have petticoats underneath and she always wears sensible shoes and carries a shawl for the chilly weather.

COUNTRY AND WESTERN

Opposite, *Black anthracite denim by Guess*
Right, *A handwoven pin-striped workshift, kerchief and soft straw hat by Polo Ralph Lauren*

DENIM

Now, denim was made to ride in not to pose around on pavements and countrygirl she don't worry too much about that little red label. Reckons it's sissy. She likes her jeans big and worked in, maybe gathered with a belt and worn with one of Grandpa's old white shirts, or a striped one. And she might wear an old straw hat to keep the flies off, or maybe not, but she always keeps great store by her kerchief (the spotted cotton kind in red or blue).

Country Photographer: Bruce Weber.
Country People: Sam Shepherd, Sissy Spacek.
Country Films: *Badlands*, *Witness*.
Country Shoe: the laced boot.
Country Hats: the cotton sprig cap, the Amish black wide-brim.
Country Details: aprons, braces, worsted stockings, no-collar shirts.

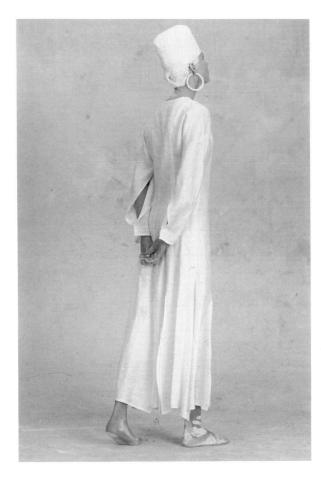

ETHNIC DRESSING

Ethnic dressing comes from the hot and sultry East whose gorgeous fabrics have been bartered and fought over for centuries by Western traders. The East has always provided an exoticism – bright Oriental silks to rich paisley and embroidered Indian shawls – to brighten the palette of Europe's dark and sombre cloth.

Ethnic dressing like the embracing of Eastern religions has also implied a rejection of the rigidity and repression of Western values. And, like the religion, is often misunderstood (try bicycling in a sari).

Modern ethnic dressing is principally about the sun and enjoying the cool unstructured clothing. It is also still about colour from the vibrant folklorics by Kenzo in the seventies to the jewel-coloured Ottoman sensuality by Rifat Ozbek in the eighties.

Take a trip.

大鸣、大放、大辩论、大字报
是毛主席倡导的四大。如有意
见或不同意见，可以文字作为
原则争论，望不得撞内擂
成覆盖满大字报！！

NORTH AFRICA/TURKEY

The North African jellaba, the Egyptian dish dash is the ubiquitous long shirt worn throughout the Arab world (not to be confused with the kaftan which has been given a bad name by opera singers in search of a bit of no-waistline glamour). Also collect from here, short embroidered jackets or waistcoats, pointed slippers and the fez.
Colours: jewel-brights, white, self-stripe, pale ochres.

CHINA

Chinese dressing is utilitarian and clean. Mao suits in working blue, crisp schoolgirl shirts with pleated skirts and red scarfs, straight trousers in black silk worn with white cotton socks and flat Chinese black plimsolls. A cap is worn at all times. In winter an indigo padded jacket. This look has no truck with Suzy Wong.

INDIA

This continent has had more sartorial woes heaped upon it than any other (remember love beads, cheesecloth and Jesus sandals?). The new hippy is in love with the textiles not the trail and collects avidly the acid orange and crimson mirrored skirts, cropped beaded shirts and as much of the ornamented silver jewellery as possible (haircombs, long earrings, plain rings, armfuls of bangles). She scours the market for fabrics to wear as throws, ornamental belts to revolutionize her urban black. She likes to wear the long cotton shirts with drawstring trousers and Nehru jacket as an alternative summer tux.

   The new hippy would never wear a turban.

INDIAN SUMMER
Above left, *Black silk shantung skirt by Emanuel with a black silk chiffon shirt by Chanel*

FOR THE ARABIAN NIGHT
Above right, *White silk organza shirt, scarlet embroidered skirt, blue silk moire cummerbund and fez – all by Rifat Ozbek*

HAT FIRST
Opposite, *White cotton toque by Graham Smith*

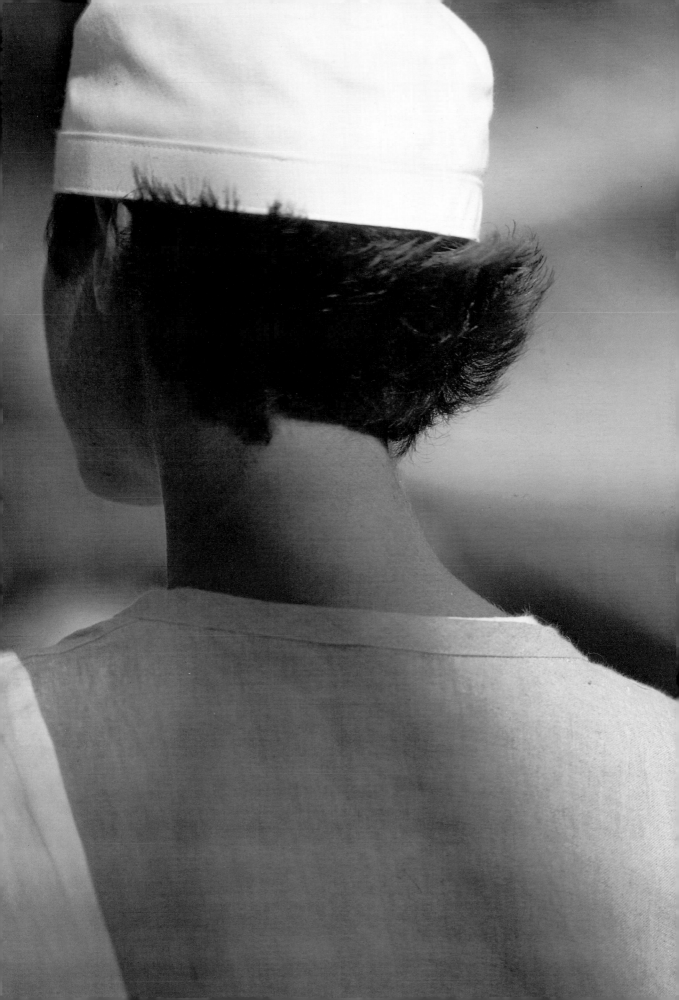

ACTION!

These are the clothes for the jumpers and jivers, the clothes that never stand still. The fashion that takes its cloth from the professional world of sport and dance but twists it into a modern spectator style.

Sport has always influenced the fashion of its day, from Victorian bicycle bloomers to Chanel's beach frocks to the contemporary Japanese gym shoe. And its primary force in each age is a sudden relaxation in clothes that never existed before – an escape from tyranny and convention. The freedom of trousers! The release from corsets! The comfort after the high heel!

Action is all about ease and simplicity from the singlet of the track to the crossover ballet cardigan. It is a no frills, no fuss, no accessory style that is about showing off the body, where the bodyline becomes the prime focus, where bareness and movement are as important as jewels to a cocktail dress.

Action is also grand leisure sport, taking all the historical romance of the hunting jacket and the skating skirt and remodelling it for practical daywear.

Whatever mode, Action loves practicality, workwear materials like cotton sweat and Lycra, and never takes anything lying down. Action is about drive and getting places. Go for it!

HIGH ENERGY
*Vests by Levi, pedal pushers in
black Lycra by Bike, and her
leather dance pumps by Gamba*

THE TRACK

Track is the fittest show-off style of them all. It's the style that sprang out of the gym right on to the pavement. Track is an aggressive urban look updated by street sports like skateboarding and park games like baseball that grew in popularity with the upsurge of fitness, especially the jogging phenomenon. It also combines an older gymnastic style from the sport-obsessed thirties, the androgynous practice suits and longlegged swimming costumes photographed so brilliantly by Hoyniugen Huené.

Track borrows its good-looking elements from all sports: the Fred Perry tennis shirt, the dual-coloured hockey shirt, the baseball jacket and hat, the old-fashioned soccer shorts, jockey silks and wrestling boots.

Mixing any of these elements with another style gives them an instant raw edge and energy.

Track Film: *Chariots of Fire*, all boxing movies.

Track Hates: sweatbands on head or wrist, pastel jogging suits, aertex, tennis no-show socks with bobbles, rugby shirts, sweatshirts with logos.

SINGLET STYLE

The singlet is the star of sports fashion. The T-shirt without arms goes with practically everything, although it needs plain colours and good shoulders. Real singlet is in cotton sweat but action girl loves it in oyster silk or pale linen for after dark.

Its cousin the long-armed **sweatshirt** is best worn *à la Américaine*,

ON THE RIGHT TRACK
Norma Kamali's singlet suit worn by itself, with bloomers or over a T-shirt. Leather ghillie shoes by Joseph

63

KEEP ON TRACKING
After the colour section,
White cotton and muslin double vest by Momento; black Lycra cycling shorts, white ankle socks, black and white cycling shoes and black patent leather helmet from W F Holdsworth

i.e. teenager style, very large and layered, sometimes with a T-shirt over the top. The sweatshirts should be in sober colour (*never* in pink or turquoise). Either alone or teamed up into the tracksuit it is best in grey or black and should only be worn inside during lazy hours or if really training. Nothing in the world looks worse than a tracksuit worn for real.

Running shorts, if worn, must be cotton or sweat. Only waiters in gay discos wear satin shorts.

Jognotes: tracksuits/tracksuit pants with T-shirt only look terrific on tall thin fit people. They may be the most comfortable notion known to modern style but *do not dupe yourself.*

BIKE STYLE

Bike style is to sex what singlet style is to comfort. The whole point of bike style is *fit* (by which I don't mean health) – the gear has got to hug the body with the tenacity of a wheel gripping the road.

Long tight black bike shorts are the great shorts of sport. They are worn with Lycra T-shirts with a good deal of racing stripe and short punchy fingerless gloves (when on a bike) and track shoes or Doc Martens. Jean Paul Gaultier became the darling of bike style when he covered his version in bold Cyrillic script.

Bikenote: bike helmets and fluorescent warning bands may be sensible for cyclists but they are no way cool. Bikers like it mean and dangerous.

TRACK SHOES

The track shoe has been walking tall in the streets this past decade in the way the high heel never could. This is not entirely unconnected with the fact that it never lets you down while running for the bus. The track shoe is guaranteed never to get stuck in escalators, to snap off, twist your ankle or slip on ice. It is, however, in the wrong context, one of the ugliest sights known to the city. Who has seen the Little Black Dress with matching Reeboks and not winced, even in NYC? One of the better aspects of the late taxi-hailing eighties is the return of the high heel to its proper place.

Nevertheless, the track shoe, in spite of a fashion for indolence, is a sports classic. No summer would be complete without an annual purchase of very plain black and white sneakers, also known as the gym shoe (with elasticated front) or the plimsoll (with laces). The essential wardrobe can never get enough. Irrespective of their cheapness, they also tend to go with everything, even adding a twist of irony to designer gear you want to play down. The navy version is the cotton deck shoe with inserts of stripe available from chandlers (not to be confused with leather topsiders). The tall plimsoll is the baseball boot, available in every colour but best in black.

Beyond Track: the cycling shoe and the boxing boot are great shapes but tend to look ridiculous unless you are *totally* serious. Anything with spikes is not advised. Anything with an aerated sole that looks as though it might go jogging is *definitely* not advised.

HUNTING

Who wants to look like a million dollars in the country? Who wants to look as though they own the country.

Hands up? Read this page.

Hunting is just about as smart and as wittily aristocratic as you can get. Even if you don't own the horse to gaze at the lesser mortals beneath, just the cut of that jacket would quell a riot. Hunting is men's dressing for women at its most traditional and successful. All that fabulous tailoring and attention to detail without appearing in the least draggy.

THE JODHPUR

Who first stole the shape of the riding breech and took it down mainstream? Probably Chanel, wise woman. The jodhpur, along with the ski pant, is one of the most flattering pant shapes, just so long as that famous outlet at the thigh is kept in control. No one wants to look like a Nazi motorcycle messenger.

Jodhpurs can be long or short. Best are the very tight cream, or the more old-fashioned khaki with turnups. All available at riding stores or sports shops.

THE HUNTING JACKET

The true hunting jacket is red (pink) which is a little show-off for Modern Style. Hunter girl takes the sharply tailored shape, nipped in the waist and all buttons up, in black and chocolate brown. Underneath, the shirt is white and starchy (see The Great White Shirt, Classics) worn with a stock in 18th-century style.

Hunt Details: string and tan leather gloves, pin brooches, stock pins, bowler hats, top hats.

Hunt Hair: sleek, bun with hairnet.

Huntjacket Alternative: The hacking jacket cut in similar shape only of tweed. The jacket worn with bustle skirt (see Edwardian, Retro).

THE RIDING BOOTS

The riding boot is the haughtiest footwear, and strides down every strada in a state of high polish. The riding boot (long) is flat, black, sometimes with a tan trim. The riding boot (short), also known as the jodhpur boot, is dark or chestnut brown with wrapover straps at the ankle. Riding boots should be tight and of the best leather. She may ride with a rubber riding boot, but she would never walk in one.

TO THE COUNTRY BORN

Opposite above, *White silk shirt and black silk tie from Chanel worn with turn-up jodhpurs*
Opposite below, *A fitted, hand-knitted navy blue cardigan with braided buttons by Marion Foale, cream stretch jodhpurs by Harry Hall and black rubber riding boots from Austin Reed*
Right, *Equestrian black wool jacket by Malvina Denler with lace jabot, bowler hat and leather gloves*

Shooting Foibles: the hat which is mad Tyrolean bristling with feathers. The walking stick. The pipe.
Shooting Colours: black, white, fawn and lots of loden green, charcoal.
Shooting Shoes: brogues and lace-up boots, white stockings.
Shooting Shots: *Mayerling*, *Last Days in Marienbad*, Christopher Plummer in *The Sound of Music*.

SHOOTING

Shooting has nothing to do with deerstalkers or beagles. Shooting is a style from another place altogether, not aristo English estate but royal European hunting lodge. An Edwardian grand style played out in the forest and mountains and possibly the best clothes of the North.

This is the look that launched Workers for Freedom, the romantic court at play in big cream shirts with stocks, buttoned dark trousers and heavy wool jackets. It borrows heavily from the Tyrolean look (but doesn't go quite as far as lederhosen), stealing its corduroy breeches, tough woollen socks, collarless jackets with horn or silver buttons, long dirndl skirts and loden capes.

When formal this style is quite military with a good deal of black and silver buttons (very Anastasia) and the hair is wildly romantic (long is possible).

THIS SPORTING LIFE
Left and above, *Modern Tyrolean Loden coats by Krauland und Sohn*
Top, *Antique bolero wool jacket with black velvet applique – all worn with felt trilbys*

FISHING

This is the charming tousled country look that had its heyday in the rural chic of the late seventies, in the days when everyone had at least one pair of corduroy trousers and two fairisles in their essential wardrobe. It is a lyrical mix of the English fly fisherman and the North Atlantic trawlerman, roughwear with good manners when the gumboot comes into its own.

Fishing layers oversize island seawools, such as Arans and guernseys, over belted, baggy rustic trousers, such as moleskin, corduroy or denim, plus an oiled jacket or short mac. Checked Viyella shirts or cotton spot scarves are worn underneath the heavy round-neck knit or long cardigan with leather buttons (never a quilted husky – fishing is no snob Sloane). Long creamy socks are worn over boots.

The Hat is a must for fishing – navy beanie, tweed or canvas fishing hat or stalker stuck with fishing flies, sou'wester, captain's hat in canvas or wool.

The Bag is intrinsic: canvas bike bag, picnic basket, leather rucksack but most of all the willow creel.

The Colours: olive *par excellence*, with natural wool, French navy and some fawn.

The Smock: where the fisherman goes sailing, the canvas seasmock is best a faded blue or Breton pink. These and matching tough trousers are available at chandlers such as Captain O. M. Watts.

Others: fingerless gloves, fresh complexion, stoic composition.

COLD COMFORT
Above, *Fur jacket with leather collar from Massa and rough knit by Ghinea*

FISHING FOR COMPLIMENTS
Opposite, *Oilskin sou'wester from Captain O. M. Watts, with Aran sweater, waders and wickerwork creel*

SNOW

Snow is when winter really likes to show off. Snow is *total* romance with winter sports, from the Russian sleds to the Tyrolean chalet (see Hunting, this chapter). It loves to wrap up in something dramatic like a fur (fake, of course) and wear different shoes inside.

Snow is also madly keen on the Olympic style of the fifties (those great ski pants!), mixed with a little roughness from early Arctic wear (those knits!). Although it must be said that it's a style that is definitely more leisure than actif, more urban than country.

Snowgirl loves a very graphic style: a wide-shouldered silhouette with long slim legs, very tall shaped hats, great swirling capes and flouncing skating skirts. And in the best winter materials, naturally, with a good deal of black so she can stand out against the snow, or rather pavement. Snowgirl wouldn't be seen dead standing out in a dayglo anorak.

Snowshoes: heavy. If nothing resembling a mountaineering boot, then a Doc Marten or a ponyskin lace-up.

Snowsatchel: the rucksack (leather, of course), old-fashioned bum bags.

Slush Items: moonboots, yetiboots, bobble hats, Davy Crockett hats, anything and everything in lime green.

SKI!

This is a look that has no truck with Gortex or the salopette. Modern Style ski is a love affair with the slopes, not a professional commitment. Modern Style ski does not hare down the *piste*, let alone the high street, in anything resembling a duvet.

This ski is a relaxed *langlauf* style, an excuse to show off the Nordic knits, the perfect pair of ski pants and an excuse to wear shades at all times. If it did wear an anorak it would be one of those long old-fashioned ones cut like a Norfolk jacket in stone gabardine.

SKI ESSENTIALS

The Balaclava. This should neither make you look like an evacuee, nor like a terrorist. The balaclava should be of thin material, worn under a tall hat, or a scarf of stretch fabric twisted into style that looks just fine with shades.

The Gloves. Woolly anything is too sweet for skigirl who is as cold as the mountain. She wraps her talons in black leather skiing gloves, or sheepskin mittens.

ICESTYLE

Opposite, *Pale pink skating skirt suit by Martine Sitbon*
Top, *Black all-in-one skating suit*
Above, *Blumarine's white angora pullover, ribbed skirt and tights*

73

SNOWSTYLE
Below, *Short black leather jacket, jersey sweater and gabardine ski pants*
Opposite, *Large Aran sweater with white cotton jersey ski pants and Argyll socks*

The Polo Neck. The white polo neck is *de rigueur* under the skiing sweater. Always in cotton.
The Shades. Mean and mirrored (see Spex, Fashion Details) or dark round goggles favoured by Scott.

THE SKI PANT

After the black polo, the ski pant is the great modern classic. With the looped-under feet, high waist and side zip, this is the most flattering stretch shape ever invented. Looks fabulous with practically everything, as long as the top is tucked in – shirts, knits, jackets, formal or informal. The ski pant must be black (pink, for instance, relegates this star to suburban slax status) and it must be of strong daywear material, although Betty Jackson once made the ski pant in glamorous crushed velvet.

A hardy fashion perennial, the ski pant appears every winter but nothing beats the real thing, at last now available at good sports shops.

NORDIC KNITS

Although pattern is a derisory notion for Modern Wool Style, the exception comes to ski. The Nordic knit is still alive with those snowflakes and reindeer, though it must be made of tough wool (nothing mimsy in mohair, certainly nothing sprinkled in lurex) and of equally tough colours (red to rust to monochrome – *no pastel*). The Nordic knit is worn as outerwear, i.e. needing no jacket. It looks best with the ski pant, in fact should only be worn with the ski pant. The designer version is usually made by Joseph, the real Icelandic found at ships' chandlers and ski stores.

ICE!

Icestyle has nothing *whatsoever* to do with spangles. It does not want to look like Torville and Dean anymore than it does a speed champion in skintight Lycra.

Icestyle is based on a civilized approach to skating, a gentle skid along the frozen canals. The most competitive icestyle gets is when it attempts to look like Sonya Henje.

Icepack: loves simple lambswool scarf to fly in the breeze with matching large gloves; knickerbockers, especially in ginger wool; elfin wool hat or cap, leather flying hat with fur-lined flaps; muffs.

THE SKATING SKIRT

The skating skirt is the ultimate dance skirt, related to the School Skirt and the Ballet Skirt and once it deviated into a sweatshirt craze called a ra-ra. The skating skirt is very, very short and needs brilliant legs to wear, plus confidence. It must flounce, flirt and stick out, preferably in a plain colour (it loves cream), and be worn with knits and thick tights. It's the mini of San Moritz.

STUDIO 1

This is a sportstyle that evolved from a romance with the dance studio that began in the late seventies with disco and rollerskating crazes and grew with the rise of aerobics and other forms of dance and exercise.

Studio 1 is all about the body showing off, the dress concepts of S-T-R-E-T-C-H and shrink. The fashion is tight-fitting, if not all over the body then on at least half, and the fabrics are hardworking – T-shirt cotton, Lycra and Spandex. It's an energetic, asexual style that combines a streamlined silhouette with clever ways of tying cloth that have arisen from reasons of comfort in extreme heat and physical exertion. Its classic statements include the leotard, leggings, sweatshirt wrap and modern dance shoe. Its designer champions range from New York power labels such as Norma Kamali to UK anarchists such as Boy and BodyMap.

JUMP!

Studio 1 Movies: *Saturday Night Fever, Flashdance, Fame!, Breakdance, Footloose.*

Leotard Heroines: Leslie Caron, Cyd Charisse.

Leotard Rebel: Michael Clark wearing BodyMap.

Beyond Leotard: Lisa Lyons.

Studio 1 Colours: tracksuit grey, T-shirt white, black (*no way anything in violet Lycra*).

Studio 1 Hair: serious amounts of headwrap, stretch headbands and high ponytails.

Studio 1 Details: high waists, thick ankle socks (no shoes), no make-up.

FOOTLOOSE AND BODY-FREE

Far left, *An easy going cut-away cotton leotard*
Left, *Body Map's stretchy striped and star-shaped knits*

ON WITH THE DANCE

Right, *Sheridan Barnett's short-legged silk crepe leotard, worn with evening gloves and high heels*

JUMP TO THE BEAT
Right, *Stirling Cooper T-bar
black jersey dress worn over a
white all-in-one jumpsuit*
Opposite above, *Azzedine
Alaia's layer of silk jersey body
over a white cotton leotard*
Opposite below left, *Comme
des Garçons' silk shirt with high-
waisted exercise tights*
Opposite below right,
*Organza wrapover shirt by
Gianfranco Ferré; ribbed cotton
legs by Norma Kamali, and silk
jersey body by Azzedine Alaia*

THE LEOTARD

The leotard is the little black dress of the studio. Long sleeved, short sleeved, no sleeve, high neck or traditional scoop neck, this ubiquitous shape crops up in every style and decade, worn always for its tightfit charm and preferably in regulation black.

Before the advent of The Body (see Undercover) the leotard was the clever way to avoid waistbunch. Looks good under most flounce skirts and straight trousers but not with classic dressing and not with jewellery.

SWEATSHIRT WRAP

Sweatshirt wrap is an anarchic attitude. It's not so much the shape (the leggings, the T-shirt, the sweatshirt) but what is done to the shape. Studio 1 massacres sweatshirt in the most aesthetic way, customizing every scrap. Leggings are shortened, T-shirts truncated, socks cut into leg warmers and arm warmers, different shapes wrapped over each other (T-shirt over sweatshirt, skirt over leggings). There is no rule except to keep cool.

THE MODERN DANCE SHOE

The modern dance shoe is the shoe to jump to. It's the flat plain ballet pump in suede, it's the character, flamenco heeled bar shoe, the metal-capped tap shoe and the demure lace-up of the studio, the jazz shoe in any colour you can think of. The modern dance shoe has no truck with ribbons or the colour pink.

At its most extreme it's a wrapped foot.

BALLETOMANE
Right, *High-waisted wool jersey trousers with shoulder straps from The Beauchamp Place Shop with an inky moiré skirt with ruched sleeves from Browns*

STUDIO 2

Studio 2 is the lyrical side of dancewear, the fragile romance of ballet mixed with raw practicality, the net skirt over the bow-necked leotard.

The essence of Studio 2 is the freedom of cloth, from sweet ballerina skirts that ripple, swish and froth to the sensuousness of the tango frock, the Little Black Dress that dances. Gigi Meets Flamenco.

AT THE BARRE

Barre bare is skinny and fawnlike. The arch of the neck and the longness of limb with no semblance of a tan. Studio 2 takes straight from class the scoop-neck and teams it with flat ballet pumps and stove-pipe trousers for the quintessential beatnik look. It takes the pale crossover cardigan mixed with soft woollens or the practice tutu for the modern Degas girl.

Barre Colours: baby blue, *eau de nil*, vanilla, shell pink.
Barre Hair: very sleek, bun or chignon, hairnets, headbands.
Barre Film: *The Turning Point.*

ON THE STAGE

This takes the ballet at its more dramatic. High-waisted black leggings, extravagant white blouses and dark velvet bodices from the male dancers (think of Robert Helpmann), the principal boy look as interpreted by Rifat Ozbek. The energy of modern formal dance, from Isadora Duncan's Grecian tunics to Martha Graham's famous bias-cut black jersey dress.

Stage Look: theatrical pallor, eyeliner, arched eyebrows (think of Margot Fonteyn in the sixties), head-dresses of velvet and feathers.
Stage Details: draped chiffon scarves, bodices and nipped waists.

ON WITH THE DANCE
Above, *A froth of silk tulle petticoats by Emanuel*

Below left, *A panelled and bias-cut black rayon crepe dress from The Beauchamp Place Shop*

Below right, *Sheridan Barnett's supple silk jersey dress*

PREPARE TO PARTY
Pout in a puffball

PARTY!

OK, you've got home, you've got out of the bath and you've got to go. Go up and go *out*. You've got to shift from day to night. PARTY! is understanding that shift, the difference between a cup of coffee and a glass of champagne. The shift from cotton and wool to more elaborate fabrics – velvet, silk, brocade. The shift from discreet accessories to a handful of show-off gems or sculptural silver. The shift in colour from sober, sensible monochrome to wild, strong colour – deepest crimson to midnight blue. The light has shifted everywhere, inside and outside, so you can afford a dramatic statement. Under the spotlight, in the candlelight, the choice of pale pink linen looks like cowardice. So on goes the make-up, up goes the hair, up go the heels and up goes the hemline (or down or out just so long as it's some direction away from the middle). You've got to treat yourself to PARTY!

The easiest, most classic, most modern detail is dare to bare. Long, deep and short cuts to reveal bare backs, bare arms, bare shoulders and legs covered in the sheerest stockings. PARTY! is about play and about sex, so you've got to show yourself off. PARTY! is also about dancing; frocks to bop till you drop in. PARTY! is about going places, looking brilliant at the opera, in the hotel, nightclubbing. PARTY! is about partying, dressing up, winter and summer, stopping work and having fun.

THE NEW COCKTAIL FROCK

The New Cocktail Frock is the six o'clock thrill, young in time and young in spirit. The New Cocktail Frock is for fun and tends to disappear in the soberer times. It is no fan of formality, would never sit down to dinner or go anywhere near a ball, loving only the years when having a good time is a priority. Then it arrives with a new name, The Sack, The Bag and The Bubble, never sensibly and always short.

The New Cocktail Frock is closely related to the Little Black Dress, except that it is never worn in daylight and is *wild* about colour – chartreuse, champagne pink, curaçao blue, white as a lady. It likes being adorned with sparkle, heavy gimmicky jewellery, feathers and amusing perching hats. It wears gloves indoors and terrifically high heels. The New Cocktail Frock is for strutting and talking and being noticed. The dress for the happy hour in every decade, whether sipping highballs or tequila slammers, this frock is flirty, frivolous and very addictive.

Cocktail Heroines: Holly Golightly, Edie Sedgwick, Betty Blue.

Cocktail Ingredients: bare arms (never tanned), sheer stockings, no handbags, hotel lobbies, limousines, laughter, mascara.

PARTY PIECES
From left to right, *Monsoon's polo-necked black velvet frock, with red feather boa and green lurex tights*
Ruched black mini with yellow boa neckline by Kahniverous
Monsoon's strapless slinky mini with ciré gloves and fishnet tights
Strapless black silk mini with orange silk sash and bow by Yves Saint Laurent

BUBBLING WITH LIFE

Left to right, *Livio de Simone's violet cotton frock hand-speckled with blue spots; hoops by Pellini and bracelets by La Medusa Ruched and puffed black and white silk bubble by Ungaro Tarlazzi's black wool jumper, black taffeta bubble and a black suede belt*

MODERN LONG
Right, *Satin body exploding
into a net frill by Biddulph
and Banham*
Opposite, *Long and lean
wool sweater over chiffon skirt
by Katherine Hamnett*

LONG AND STRONG

Now, Long can go very wrong or can come very expensive, preferring as it does tons of taffeta to a moderate amount of cotton. Long is as modern as you make it – you don't always have to look like a Sloane at a Farmer's Ball or an argument with the sewing machine. If the occasion fits, wear it and wear it grandly. The point about Long has nothing to do with cool but to do with reserve.

OLD GOLD

The dressing-up box is brilliant for Long. Glamour gowns are not hard to find in good second-hand shops or new hire shops. Look for Balenciaga black, thirties bias cut or fifties New Look. Resist the temptation to look as though you belong to a TV serial or are about to walk up the aisle. Old Gold Long may wear the past but it is never fancy dress. You've got to think gracious to get away with it. Sedate walk, hair up (the neck and shoulders are v. important to Long), lots of paste, good manners and satin slippers at all times. An Old Gold does not like an anorak slung casually over it like an anti-hero. If you haven't a cape wear a shawl or a piece of contrasting heavyweight material (*no crochet*).
Designer Debutante: Grace Kelly in *High Society*.

MODERN LONG

Modern Long is not a frock. Modern Long is strong on top and weak at the knees, i.e.

JEWEL IN THE GOWN
Opposite, *Strapless cream silk long dress with gold and diamante beadwork by Victor Edelstein*

SKIRTING THE ISSUE
Right, *White silk organza halter-necked dress with a froth of ballerina skirts by Paul Golding Couture*

separates with mixed textures. Perfect sweaterdressing on top (long tunic, palest twinset) with fragile skirts of chiffon, organza or lace, something that blows in the breeze, most wittily executed by Comme des Garçons where Long became charming rather than stuffy.

Modern Long Loves Certain Colours: Jasper Conran's coffee-coloured chiffon, Georgina von Etsdorf's blue and violet flower print. Luckily for party girl young, inexpensive designers use a lot of artificial fibres that don't show with the night lights.

Modern Long Goes Ethnic: the great summer alternative is the sarong, whether simply itself in patterned silk or cleverly constructed in plain by Rifat Ozbek. It replaces sweaterdressing with silk dressing (see Classics) and piles on the silver and amber.

NB: Modern Long is casual but seriously immaculate. Long, whatever style, always gets into taxis and *never* runs for the bus.

ROMANTIC

In every age there is a Romantic mode. Cleopatra storms the stage yet there is always Ophelia floating in the weed-locked lake; even if Odile gets to dance then Odette still hovers in the wings.

The Romantic party mode is worn by an ethereal modern, the antithesis of the vamp. She is very English, very silent, a lover of ballet (see Studio 2, Action!) and ghost stories – a mixture of faery and consumptive. She is Beatrice painted by Rossetti, the smudge-eyed girl photographed by Sarah Moon dressed in Biba, the Empire girl celebrated in chiffon by Romeo Gigli, the disturbed angel designed by John Galliano.

This party girl smiles but wanly.

Romantic Shape: loose, free, unstructured. The Romantic is pale and flat-chested and simply adores the medieval period.

Romantic Fabric: natural, always plain. Restrained silk, muslin.

Romantic Colours: smoke, plum, mushroom, dead white.

Romantic Accessories: hair bound in coils and curls, plaited or loose (if it's short, it will be the Joan of Arc cut). A bonnet in springtime, sweet silver jewellery and very little make-up. If she could, this party girl would carry a few lilies where most would hold a glass of champagne.

Romantic Yearnings: Camille, daybeds, hooded capes (as seen in *The French Lieutenant's Woman*), ruins, practically all 19th-century poetry.

SHADES OF THE MEDIEVAL COURT
Opposite, *Royal blue crushed velvet coat worn with pearl, enamel and lapis lazuli*
Right, *Pastel-coloured crushed silk dresses by Made in Italy*

THE ALTERNATIVE TUX

The Alternative Tux is the party girl who doesn't want to wear a frock. The party girl who likes to *flâner* the boulevard and throw open the double doors. The Alternative Tux is not a style for the sweet or fainthearted, nor even for the wicked temptress. It needs a boyish flamboyance to carry it perfectly.

The Alternative Tux can be a classic – a man's dinner jacket with satin lapels or a smoking jacket. This tux is worn with a shirt (piqué plain, ruffled, winged, embroidered but always white). Baggy trousers are held up with old coloured felt or braided Tyrolean braces. Severity is banished with wild wearing of costume jewellery: fake rubies, emeralds and ropes of pearl. Plus a nonchalant display of lace jabot or clashing chiffon scarf about the neck and a cummerbund about the waist (stolen from the boys or a scarf cleverly doubled). Dark-coloured waistcoats, pale silk waistcoats, decorated waistcoats are collected and worn, sometimes by themselves, oversized with floppy collared shirt. This classic tux doesn't need a bow tie (you don't want to be mistaken for the waiter). A diplomatic medal never goes amiss.

The modern classic tuxes can be fifties rock jackets worn with black ski pants and polo necks, a uniform jacket (not too bandboy) or a stern black jacket with Nehru collar. The Alternative Tux can even be a coat so long as it is a dandy coat made of a night-time fabric.

Tux Steps: The Alternative Tux likes its shoes to toe tap. Soft leather knee boots, suede pixie or patent buckled pumps or velvet monogrammed slippers. It wouldn't be seen dead with high heels.

THEATRICAL TUX

The Theatrical Tux is the rakish dandy coat that swaggers through the night with a mental walking cane. It is an 18th-century court suit worn with breeches, silver buttons and extravagant cuffs. It is Watteau-inspired costume in clown whites and pale blues and lots of organza. It is a frockcoat, even a tailcoat, as long as it's worn with a frill and skinny dancing legs.

Coatnote: the coatdress of the evening is often found in theatre sales, textile and costume shops. The fabric should always be dramatic, a strong rich colour such as crimson, or a ghostly pale such as oyster or ivory. Best in black velvet. Long dinner jackets (from thrift stores) are a good alternative.

Frockcoat Designer Darling: Jean Paul Gaultier.

THE EIGHTEENTH-CENTURY DANDY

Above, *Ivory silk shantung coat by Wendy Dagworthy, pale organza shirt by John Galliano, cream moiré jodhpurs by Vanilla – with antique brocade and kid gloves*
Opposite, *Pale pink cotton coat by Nigel Preston; white doubled organza shirt by Yohji Yamamoto; white silk wrapover skirt by Comme des Garçons – and a fine layer of white silk tulle*

ETHNIC TUX

The Ethnic Tux is inspired by the formal wear from other countries, from wintertime austere Austrian wool to summertime light silken Chinese. Its main forms are:

The Scottish Dancing Rig: dark cropped jacket, preferably in velvet with sharp tartan trousers or short kilt.

The Indian Gentleman: biscuit linen Nehru jackets with muslin tops or long Indian cotton shirts, white leggings and sandals.

The Matador: for cropped bolero and high waist trousers see Spanish Style in Another Country.

ALTERNATIVE TUX
Right, *Nehru-collared black velvet by Mark and Syrie*
Opposite, *Fine filigree frock coat in black velvet by Onix*

UNDERCOVER

These are the hidden clothes, the clothes you keep closest to you that nevertheless may be on show. Undercover is about keeping plain and basic underneath with the purest possible fabrics (cotton, crêpe de Chine and silk) with the simplest, surest shapes. Undercover takes you from the modern athletic bra to the historical camisole, from French knickers to the new American Y-front.

Undercover answers essential questions for what to wear at night. Is there a renaissance of the baby doll? Does the modern girl ever wear bedsocks? Does she keep her kimono just for show?

Undercover is about the modest underwear that doubles as showoff outerwear. The modern leggings that came from Grandad's combinations, the velvet bustier that came from Grandma's cotton corset. The white vest that turned into a singlet, the man's silk pyjamas that turned into a clever shirt.

Undercover reveals all.

**UNDERCOVER
EXPOSÉ**
High-cut cotton pants by Joseph

**BARE
ESSENTIALS**
Opposite, *White silk
bra and boxer
shorts by Sami*
Right, *Pink silk
crépe de chine
camiknickers by
La Verne Preston*

BASICS

There are many things we have to thank the 20th century for and one of them is underwear. Just think of the machinations a girl formerly had to go through just to get dressed! The liberty bodice must be one of history's great misnomers. Basic underwear has nothing to do with lingerie, particularly the skimpy sort in black lace that men are supposed to buy for their wives at Christmas.

Basic underwear is for a modern independent, not for a calendar fantasy. And the modern independent likes everything plain and simple, whether in white cotton or oyster silk (for it has to be said, although practicality is the order of the day, no one should be afraid of a little *luxe*).

Basically, no amount of nostalgia would induce the modern independent to wear that winter vest with sleeves again. She might wear

the singlet as a vest which is fine, or a white T-shirt in cold weather. She also might wear some thermals if it gets very brisk but she wouldn't show these off. Who wants to look like Grandpa on the beach? Especially in the bedroom.

Basic Shop: who doesn't buy theirs at Marks and Spencer?

Basic Heroes: Calvin Klein, who first put a girl in a Y-front. Jasper Conran, who brought her back to crêpe de Chine.

Basic Heroines: Elizabeth Taylor in *Cat On A Hot Tin Roof*.

Basic Dilemmas: *Q*. What is my position on French knickers? *A*. OK if you're not wearing anything else. *Q*. Do I invest in a slip? *A*. Depends on how many unlined skirts you have. *Q*. Do I buy anything in nylon? *A. Never*.

Basic Hates: Knickers-in-a-bag, paper knickers, red knickers, shop assistants who insist on giving advice on you and your brassière, padded bras for teenagers, Edwardian underwear worn seriously.

IN BRIEF
Above, *White satinized boxer shorts by Sulka*
Opposite, *White cotton pants by Christies*

THE BODY

While the boxer short was the great undercover story for men in the eighties, women stole the show with the Bodysuit. The Body, similar to the teddy *sans* frills, is the all-in-one undergarment that no modern girl can live without. The Body combines sex with practicality and is one of the most vital and versatile ingredients of essential wardrobe. You can wear the Body by day, you can wear it by night, you can wear it in bed. Just so long as you remember that this garment is for show, and for wearing with proper clothes. The Bodysuit

is all about avoiding any bump at the waistline. It's as streamlined as Concorde and it can take practically any shape as long as it's *tight*. It likes a polo neck, a boat neck, even a collar, it likes no sleeve, long sleeve, even a cap sleeve but when it comes to colour it's a little more particular, preferring the monochromes and urban browns – chocolate, taupe and mushroom. A Body would look very silly in sugar pink.

Bodysuit Hero: Azzedine Alaia.

Bodysuit Alternatives: the leotard, the swimming costume.

UNDERWEAR AS OVERWEAR

The first underwear that appeared as outerwear must have been the peeping hemline of the Regency pantaloon. Since then underwear hasn't been able to resist showing itself to the outside world, from the slip-as-dress to vest-as-singlet.

The historical under-overwear has always been from our Victorian inheritance. There is practically no market or second-hand store that doesn't carry at least one rack of white cotton camisoles, petticoats and bloomers. Whereas a cautious mix of this and accompanying lace with some strict tailoring is still modern, taking the whole thing seriously will make anyone look like a dated milkmaid.

The contemporary flirtation is with the corset, from Thierry Mugler's wasp-waisted belts to Vivienne Westwood's pink satin 'Statue of Liberty' bodice. Here the corset is worn by itself or with a voluminous organza shirt for a dramatically defined waist. Although the corset is real sex-dressing, resist the temptation to labour the point by putting it together with very tight, black, or leather clothes. You don't want to look like a *maîtresse*.

Stockings, after years of the nylon pair-of-tights, have also appeared in the essential wardrobe, from opaque cotton to ultra sheer and as long socks, showing the bare gap between the insouciance. The very long (plain) sock is worn like the thigh boot, with a flourish. Looking good with very short skirts and the new wave hot pant, it is a key item for School Dressing.

Fashion Victim Under-over Wear: Jean Paul Gaultier's velvet whipped cornet bra frocks.

Short Summer: alternative shorts – men's boxers.

INSIDE OUT

Below, *Brocade corset and suspender skirt; a cotton T-shirt and mini – all by Claire Sharp*
Below right, *Pearly satin and silk camisole by Valentino*
Opposite, *Yards of chiffon with a peach satin three-quarter-length bra from Rigby and Peller*

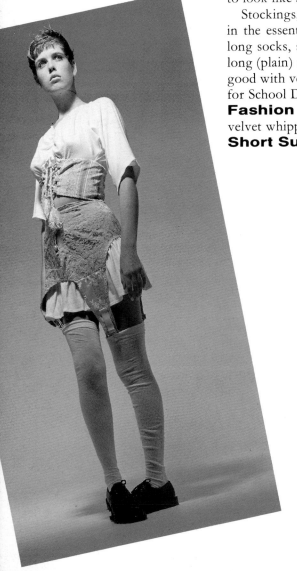

NIGHT WEAR

M odern night is Marilyn Monroe sleeping in nothing but Chanel No. 5. But sometimes a pyjama top can have its own charm and not every corridor is centrally heated. So if you are tired of the ubiquitous long T-shirt, but don't want to look like Auntie, read on for the essential sleepstyle guide.

THE PYJAMA

The Pyjama stolen from the boys, rediscovered by Margaret Howell in the early eighties, is the great modern classic of the bedroom. And not only there, for the Pyjama (especially the top) in cream or pale pink piped silk or sea island cotton is worn at the best outings as the casual Alternative White Shirt.

Remember Pyjama parties and all that lounging about in hotel suites in the thirties? Well, that's the kind of Pyjama Modern Style likes – the kind that prefers a highball to a cup of cocoa.

Of course, there is the Country Pyjama that has no inkling of sophistication. This is the pair that you save for cold, damp, windy houses, winter cottages and the 'flu days. Borrowed from the boys, it is candy-striped in faded school colours, while the girl's version is in sweet rose sprig. Whatever, the key word is Viyella and no one and nothing can beat it for cosy factor.

Night owl, though she may toy with the idea of bringing back

(ironically) the baby dolls and mules, has no intention of wearing anything called a 'nightie', especially those that envelop the body from head to toe and have elasticated cuffs. Night-time may be for sleep but it's also for sex and who wants to make love to a beanbag in flannel?

No, night owl sticks to her favourite T-shirt for this section, or an old-fashioned night shirt (just so long as it isn't in convict stripes).

Night Owl Screeches: negligées (especially in coffee edged with cream lace), bedsocks, bedjackets (anything knitted especially for bed, if cold wear an old cream cardigan), cold cream.

THE DRESSING GOWN

You think of the Dressing Gown and you think of Noël Coward lounging about with cigarettes and clever quips. So who wrote anything witty for the woman in wincyette? All the grand statement dressing gowns are for the men, Sherlock Holmes smoking velvet and extravagant amount of paisley silk in deep golds and crimsons, all that decadence (meanwhile women steal their more sober paisley cottons and tartans with silken tasselled cords and wear them *sweetly*!).

Still, when it comes to Modern Style, all is equality with the towelling dressing gown (long for men, short for women) in the richest, thickest white you can afford. Remember the nicest sight in the world? Two long strong towelgowns on the back of the hotel bathroom door. The one you're not paying for.

Dress Down: housecoats in quilted nylon, slippers lined with sheepskin, everything in candlewick.

Dress Ethnic: the Japanese kimono in old violet silk for showing off (watch those sleeves in the coffee) or indigo cotton for practical summers. Never a black nylon Happi coat from Hong Kong.

NIGHTOWLS
Opposite, *Floral print Viyella pyjama pants by Margaret Howell and grey wool cardigan by Yohji Yamamoto*
Below left, *Blue satin dressing gown by Tuttabankem with ivory satin pyjamas by James Drew*
Below, *Man's striped Viyella pyjamas with a plaid woollen dressing gown*

WEATHER DRESSING

Winter is about wrap-up in all the great English fabrics of tartans and wools, Arans and jerseys. Winter is about the cleverness of layering one fabric over another and still looking cool.

Winter looks good in the city, from the long sootblack coat to the urban hip of the leather jacket and the new wave patterned wools. Winter looks good in the country, with gritty woollens and old sheepskins and rustic colours: heathery tweeds, stone gabardine, navy wool.

Summertime is the time to undress. Time to throw away the heaviness and discover the freedom of one-layer clothes and the simplicity of the great white T-shirt. Summer is summer holiday and country weekends: linens for the garden and sundresses for the beach. Summer is about bare skin, straw hats and sandals.

It begins with the spring duster coat and ends with putting away the swimsuit for another year.

Start here . . .

THE GREAT COVER-UP
Yohji Yamamoto's grey wool coat, jodhpurs, cap and rubber wedged boots

THE WHITE STUFF
*Overleaf, left to right,
Jean Paul Gaultier's dress and coat-jacket
Sonia Rykiel's trouser suit
Azzedine Alaia's safari jacket*

115

LINEN DRESSING

L inen is the star fabric of summer. Looking the epitome of cool and calm while everybody else overheats. Small wonder the empire loved it so (see Edwardian, Retro). Linen dressing begins with the linen suit, tailored but loose, and practically always in cream or white with long jacket and tucked trousers. The linen suit loves the great white shirt and a drift of organza scarf. It can just get away with the panama.

The duster coat is the coat for spring, when it's too cool to go without and too warm and light to bring out winter coat. The duster is a loose long linen shift of a coat that loves pale colours: almond pink, stone, fawn, and worn in the same spirit as the light breezy trench mac. The duster looks best with classic linen or cotton pants. Linen dressing goes more déshabillé with the long linen skirt, worn with sandals and abandoned sweater dressing. Although it also looks good prim and pleated in white or Prince of Wales check (see Twenties, Retro), as long as it's practically full length worn *à la* Deauville with long cream and navy cotton knits or blazers.

Linen Designer Stars: Jasper Conran (the skirts), old Margaret Howell.

Sports Linen: crisp tailored city shorts, the linen singlet.

School Linen: the pleated linen gym slip, worn with short-sleeved shirt.

COOL CUTS
Opposite left, *Margaret
Howell's sleeveless white linen
shirt worn with a silk chiffon
dirndl*
Opposite right, *Ralph
Lauren's white linen breeches
with a charcoal linen duster
coat by Matsuda*
Right, *Blue and white sailor
suit by Taylor Brothers*

SWEET FROCKS OF SUMMER
Left, *Flower-sprigged mini shift*
Opposite, *Chintz fitted and flared frock by Laura Ashley*

THE SUNDRESS

The Sundress is the sweet frock of summer. It is the nice sister of the Little Black Dress. It doesn't have a mean or wicked thread anywhere.

The Sundress comes in many shapes – a sixties A-line to an unstructured long shift. It comes in many colours: faded blues and apricots, pale chintz, jewelled red, even black. The uniting theme is bare: the Sundress cannot have sleeves. A summer dress may have sleeves but even if it has the tiniest hint of a cap sleeve it won't ever be a Sundress. The Sundress also would never be seen with stockinged legs. It loves bare legs (tanned if possible) and bare feet that like to walk through the sand.

This is the frock of the resort and promenade that goes abroad when it can, and never strays far from the sea.

Sundress Hats: white sunhats, bashed straw.

Sundress Clouds: the accessory. Can't be bothered with watches or jewellery, except perhaps the odd plain silver bangle (all that swimming). The only rock the sundress likes is for sitting on.

SUNSTROKES
Left, *Chloe's long bias-cut silk print*
Below, *Thierry Mugler's A-line black cotton*
Opposite, *Ralph Lauren's floral cotton sarong*

ON THE BEACH
Left to right, *Bermudas in silver silk lamé by Zoran Handknitted cotton culotte suit by Muriel Grateau Stretchy tangerine vest and black micro-mini by Stirling Cooper*

BEACHWEAR

Beachwear is the most casual wear of the essential wardrobe. Nothing would induce beachgirl to go to work; she is pure sun, sand and fun, born with a surf song in her head and a bottle of Clarins Suntan Lotion Factor 2 in her hand. Modern beachgirl is quite a tomboy, sportif rather than decoratif, preferring a pair of pure white plimsolls to a pretty pair of sandals. She loves beachcomber hats, faded cotton, loose white shirts and the darkest tan.

THE WHITE T-SHIRT

Every beachgirl has the key kit: paperback, shades, towel and the great white T-shirt. The easiest item to find, beachgirl constantly looks for the perfect one as the surfer does the perfect wave, neither too small nor too large with the correct length sleeves and right scoop of neck. The best T-shirts are American and sometimes have the three-buttoned front. Beachgirl will knot her T-shirt and roll its sleeves for a tighter sexier fit. She will not tolerate it when it has gone washing machine grey, and only allows certain ideological messages in strict typeface to mar the front, if at all; certainly no logos.

Very First T-shirt: Marlon Brando in *On The Waterfront.*
Honorary White T-shirt: the black T-shirt.

SHORTS

Beachshorts have no relation to the slickly pressed city shorts that favour navy and a leather belt. Beachshorts are rough and ready from short tracksuit monochromes to long regulation khaki. Beachshorts love the faded look and their greatest fabric is the cut-off denim, ripped, fraying and bleached by sun and salt (which cannot resist coming to town dressed wickedly with tailored jacket and great white shirt).

Beachshorts do not, however strong the retro urge, feel the need to go Hawaiian bermuda. It's not OK for suntan oil and it's not OK for the shorts (shirts maybe). Only Elvis Presley looked OK in the floral beanie.

BEACHBABIES
Left, *Black cotton singlet worn over white cotton jersey by Katherine Hamnett*
Opposite, *Black T-shirting tunic by Comme des Garçons*

SWIMSUIT

After years of domination by the bikini, the swimming costume finally emerged from the locker as the indispensable cover-up for beach and pool in the eighties. The modern swimsuit plays with form as the dolphin does the sea: it is severely plain and black, it flirts with a skirt, it has thin straps, thick straps, one strap or no straps, it can even have legs like a bicyclist's shorts. It can be sharp and racy or pretty and pouting. Whatever, this swimsuit likes to be noticed.

Bikini Note: the modern bikini is worn separately, the never-too-skimpy top with a beach sarong, and the bikini bottom as-skimpy-as-you-like with tan oil. The great advantage of the bikini over the swimsuit is the stomach factor. For those who love to bare some restrained midriff, the wideband bikini with shorts legs is a must.

REGULATION

The Regulation costume is the plain little black swimsuit once reviled, with memories of school races and over-chlorinated pools. Now this simple black shape is celebrated on every swank beach and poolside as the modern waterbaby classic.

The little black swimsuit loves a crossover back and a high or a small scooped front. It does not understand the concept of a radically plunged back or décolleté front. The only plunge it likes is into the sea.

Regulation Alternative Colour: flannel grey.
Historical Regulation: the black swimming costume with legs from the twenties and thirties.
Regulation Designer Stars: BodyMap.

RETRO

The Retro costume is practically a frock. It loves the frilly fifties costume with smocked front and cotton flower prints. It loves the forties wrapover-cut costume worn by Hollywood starlets. In fact the Retro costume thinks it's constantly in a bio-pic, the star of every Tarzan episode and surf film.

Retro Heroine: Brigitte Bardot.

Retro Accessories: the Retro costume is the one form of swimwear that cries out for make-up and heels. Otherwise winged shades, cartwheel hats and pale skin (retroswimmer is far too busy posing to get a suntan).

SPORTIF

The Sportif costume flourishes every four years when the Olympic swimmers spring on to the screen and everyone practises their butterfly.

The Sportif costume doesn't mess with detail or worry about looking good on the beach, it's too busy swimming. It's made of serious streamlined Lycra, is cut high on the hip and low down the back for perfectly honed bodies. The Sportif colours tend to be loud (for standing out in lane), scarlet, lime or racing stripes.

Sportif Label: Speedo.

Sportif Accessories: the towel slung round neck, the swimming cap, goggles, underwater watch.

FOR THE FAST LANE
Above left, *Liza Bruce's white cotton swimsuit with T-back*
Above, *Azzedine Alaïa's white cotton and Lycra one-piece with crossover back*
Opposite, *Comme des Garçons' grey T-shirting swimsuit, fronded cotton towelling robe with hood and linen scarf*

THICK KNITS
Opposite, *Marion Foale's
handknit: a collared sweater
in tough grey wool*
Right, *Thick knit polo-neck
sweater by Kenzo*

KNITS

The knits of winter are tough and brought up in the country. They can be long and plain or short and patterned but they must be chunky, must be wool and must not be confused with sweater-dressing (see Classics) which is altogether a different concept, and very urban.

Winter knit can be a hipknit, the knit of the season so long as it's quite restrained. Winter knit would never wear anything with bobbles swinging from it or logos in lurex.

Winter Knit Star: the fairisle which suffered terribly from its Hovis bread image, now making a comeback. But never in pastel.

Winter Knit Designer Stars: Marion Foale, Edina Ronay.

Winter Knits Knots: Army jumpers with leather patches on the elbows, shocking pink, Icelandic jumpers with animals, tank tops.

TRAD KNITS

Traditional jerseys are knitted with seawool. The cold-cheating wools of the fishing communities each with their own distinct patterns, the most famous being the Aran (cream) and the guernsey (navy). The

guernsey has suffered from being labelled Sloanewear but the Aran has not lost favour, especially among young British designers who love to weave and chop it in different ways.

The trick with trad knits is either not to be swamped by them (buy a child's size) or to be completely swamped by them (buy a man's size). Just baggy will not do.

Others include the patterned classic, the jewel-coloured intarsia (worn small, not *à la* golfing), and the collared games sweater in cream or gymslip grey.

Aran Designer Hero: John Galliano.
Intarsia Designer Heroine: Georgina Godley.

THE CARDIGAN

This is the cardigan that is long and strong in lambswool, the traditional deep V neck with buttons, or in thick ribbed wool with leather buttons worn as a wool jacket. This is the cardigan loved by writers (think of Hemingway) and gardeners (think of Vita Sackville West). This cardigan loves classic casuals, long pleated skirts and classic pants in wool or gabardine, with white shirts or polo shirts. The cardigan is best in sombre colours: fawn, honey, charcoal, navy or black. The thicker version takes a gritty wool.

WINTER COAT

The winter coat is the show-off and the hide-all of winter. Less formal than the classic coat (see Classics) it doesn't die for double-breasted perfection, taking its cut instead from outsider influences from the naval jacket to the motorcycle jacket. The most redoubtable form is the outsize tweed coat, usually bought second-hand. Otherwise essential wardrobe grabs . . .

URBAN BLACK

The Urban Black coat changes with the season. It takes a forties cut, an astrakhan collar, a swirling coat length, sometimes it pretends to be a jacket. But it is always there, in sombre wool, designer, retro or thrift. No pavement is without this funereal silhouette.

THE DUFFLE

The Duffle, despised for years as the uniform for schoolbrats and woolly-hatted 'radicals', has finally won favour again as a coat of hip. Worn as in early sixties movies in baggy fawn or naval cream, the Duffle is the ubiquitous casual. Never wear it too tight, never wear it in regulation navy.

Duffle Film: *The Cruel Sea*.
Duffle Designer Stars: Paul Smith, Jean Paul Gaultier.

WRAP IT UP
Left to right, *Black wool
Muscovite with astrakhan cuff
and collar; Sheepskin bomber
jacket by Fratelli Gallotti;
Scarlet anorak in parachute silk
by Katherine Hamnett*

137

OUTDOOR GIRLS
Opposite, *Single-breasted
herringbone coat from Hackett,
white woollen sweater and
cardigan by Marion Foale*
Right, *Man's duffle coat by
Sospetto with a sweater by
Creativity*

THE NEW ANORAK

The new anorak never went fishing or skiing. No, the daddy of this
baby was the mod's own parka, redesigned in brilliant silken hues by
Katherine Hamnett (*sans* furry hood). Always extravagant with colour
and texture and size, the new anorak would go to almost any length to
get rid of its dull khaki inheritance.

THE LEATHER JACKET

This is, with the 501s, the modern classic of all time, less of a coat,
more of a way of life. It is the jacket of cool. Who do you think of
with the leather jacket? Marlon Brando in *The Wild One*. James Dean
in everything. Need one say more?

The leather jacket, however, should not be too heavy or butch, more
of a moped jacket than a motorcycle jacket. Unless, of course, there is
a motorcycle. It is best in plain glove leather, collarless and cropped,
and black every time. Its soul brother is the suede jacket in honey or
tobacco brown.

Second-hand Classic: the American flying jacket (don't say
Chuck Yeager to leather jacket).

Let it be understood that Retrodressing has nothing to do with dressing up. It does not wallow in nostalgia wishing *if only* it had been born in a different decade and got to smoke cigarettes in long tortoiseshell holders with impunity. There is one thing worse than a fashion victim and that is a retro fashion victim.

Retrodressing is about borrowing certain key items and styles from the past, without being slavishly copy cat or looking like a spare part from a costume drama. Each age borrows from another and will interpret it in another way: the Regency love of the Empire Line was entirely different from that recreated by Romeo Gigli and John Galliano. Jasper Conran's Jackie O fifties and Katherine Hamnett's Emma Peel sixties could never have been worn by the original models. The first secret is to nick and mix. It is not necessary to take the Whole Look but mix a retro frock from the thirties with modern Doc Martens, an Edwardian fichu with strict eighties tailoring. The past revitalizes any wardrobe: the rediscovery of crushed velvet, amber beads, a way to twist a scarf, old prints or even a beret worn differently.

The second secret is to read the mood of the moment, have your finger on the historical pulse. This changes every season as designer stars change each season (once Chanel prêt, then all the couturiers in Paris). Keep eyes scoured in the marketplace. Modern Girl cannot afford to get vaseline on her wide-angle lens.

RETRO DRESSING

AS YEARS GO BY
Geraldine Chaplin in White Mischief

AFTER A FASHION
Above, *Meryl Streep in* Out of Africa

EMPIRE LINE
Below, *White linen pleated peplum jacket and fan-tail bustle skirt by Lesley Gale*

AFRICAN QUEEN
Below right, *Pale green tailored suit by Martine Sitbon*

MODERN EDWARDIAN
Opposite, *Old straw hat with yellow and violet flowers, crumpled brown trench, and antique ivory silk and lace*

EDWARDIAN EMPIRE

In spite of every criticism, England is still in love with its golden imperial summer, the summer of sailor suits, perfectly pressed lawns and laundry, and Big Hats. The Edwardian period is the most nostalgic period of them all (except perhaps American in the fifties), and love of its style has existed in each subsequent decade from the Laura Ashley high-necked blouse in the seventies to Katherine Hamnett's bustle skirts in the eighties.

This is the look of easy civilization. This is not a street look, you do not want to look like someone hot off the set of *Oliver!*, rather a cool detached guest at a garden party, cricket match or Oxford picnic.

Linen is the key to the Edwardian summer (never winter, for winter is too bitterly realistic). Long cool biscuit linens: three-quarter jackets in polite colours (pale mauve, lemon yellow), with drop piped collars or sailor collars; long narrow skirts worn with white or cream silk shirts and lace and long fitted coats with narrow sleeves and shoulders (the Edwardian girl never works out). Plus a borrowing of the men's veranda look: linen suits, panama hats, cravats and canvas shoes.

Edwardian Hats: large straw, brimming with garden flowers and beehive veils.

Edwardian Details (girls): the lace jabot and fichu, hat pins, tie pins, jet, cameo, chiffon scarves (especially by Georgina von Etsdorf), plain kid or lace gloves, parasols.

Edwardian Details (men's): wing collars, white gloves, fob watches, cloaks, canes, handkerchiefs.

Edwardian Hair: chignon or French pleat.

Edwardian Shoe: the button boot.

Edwardian Shorts: bloomers.

Edwardian Screen: practically every TV costume drama of which *Upstairs, Downstairs* is seminal. Plus *Jewel in the Crown* (Edwardian girl would have loved to have lived in India), *The Go-Between*, *My Fair Lady* (Cecil Beaton, designer shooting star), *Death in Venice*.

Edwardian Authors: E. M. Forster, Marcel Proust.

Edwardian Places: Florence, Brighton, Baden-Baden.

Edwardian Photographer: Henri Lartigue.

THOROUGHLY MODERN STYLE

This page, *Margaret Howell's crisp and tailored white linen shirt and jacket*
Opposite top, *Louise Brooks with brother Ted in Hollywood, 1928*
Opposite left, *Black-and-white check pleated skirt by Sheridan Barnett, a man's shirt from Paul Smith, with a white cashmere cardigan and black straw cloche*
Opposite right, *Unflappable: All-white linen skirt by Margaret Howell and cashmere twinset by N. Peal*

ROARING TWENTIES

The twenties was the era of the first modern girl, who cut her hair, threw away her corset and danced till dawn in her new cocktail dress.

The twenties was also the era of the first serious sportswear, invented, like the suntan, by Chanel. Twenties style is languorously sportif, taking the long pleated skirts from the tennis court and the deep V-necked sweaters from cricket and every combination of navy and white from yachting. At night, it returns to the jazz age in drop-waisted flapper silk with a string of impossibly long pearls and a possible amount of highballs.

Flapper Colours: neutrals, pale pink, French navy, stripes.
Flapper Films: *The Great Gatsby, Paper Moon, The Boyfriend, The Sting.*
Flapper Author: Colette.
Flapper Hair: the bob.
Flapper Shoe: the bar shoe.

Flapper Hat: the cloche.
Flapper Heroes: Noël Coward, Josephine Baker.
Flapper Places: Nice, Cannes, Deauville (the twenties was when the beach was at its most chic).
Flapper Details: silk stockings.

THIRTIES DUSTBOWL

GO WEST YOUNG WOMAN
Above, *Sally Field in* Places in the Heart
Below, *Spare and simple Sunday best from Sonia Rykiel*
Below right, *Washday blue and white polka-dot frock with a cravat collar from Liette*
Opposite, *Down on the Farm: A faded flower-sprigged chiffon wrap and frock*

While Europe partied in pale bias-cut frocks on cruises and in Berlin nightclubs, there was a more realistic style in the Depression-hit states of America. The dustbowl look is a romantic glance at the hard-working fierce women migrating from the ruined wheat-fields to the fruit orchards of California. It's America celebrating its pioneer spirit in frocks.

While the men wear overalls and dungarees, the women wear faded cotton or crêpe, long flowerprint dresses with plain collars and short sleeves. Dustbowl girl is rawboned, serious and freckled, with bare legs and no make-up. She wears peep-toed sandals or sensible lace-ups (usually one size too large) with ankle socks. When the wind blows she puts on a short granny cardigan.

Dustbowl Movies: *Grapes of Wrath, The River, Places of the Heart.*
Dustbowl Hat: broken wide-brimmed straw sunhat.
Dustbowl Hair: chopped boyish bob, or scraped-back ponytail.
Dustbowl Designer Star (grandstyle): Georgina von Etsdorf.

Dustbowl Photographers: Walker Evans, Paul Strand.
Dustbowl Painters: Georgia O'Keeffe, Andrew Wyeth.
Dustbowl Places: Oklahoma.

146

AIR RAID FORTIES

The forties look is quintessential England, an England of plummy accents, bonhomie and cardigans that existed in an unconvincing village set built by Ealing Studios. This is the look that expects the vicar for tea and is frightfully good at riding a bicycle.

Forties girl simply adores a plain white shirt with puffed sleeves (so sensible), tweed suits with nipped waists and stiff upper shoulders and the twinset (with pearls). She wears thick wool stockings with brogues and always carries a crocodile handbag. She adores her Oxford bags (the forties is the peak era for classic pants).

Forties girl (French version) is less tweedy and less jolly. This is Resistance chic that expects the padre and rides the bicycle for entirely different reasons. Resistance girl wears black for cover: plain jersey, pleated skirts with ankle socks and clumpy shoes. She wouldn't go anywhere without her beret or her trench.

Both English and French wartime girls take austerity to its limits.

WOMEN AT WAR
Opposite, *Land Girl:* *Armani's grey herringbone tweed Oxford bags with turn-ups and a cashmere twinset by Pringle*
Above, *Faye Dunaway*
Below, *Resistance Chic: White linen shirt, blue cashmere V-neck and grey herringbone tweed pleated skirt – all by Ralph Lauren*
Below left, *Country Chic: Brown tweed check jacket and skirt by Sheridan Barnett*

Wartime Magazine: *Picture Post.*
Wartime Details: corsage, nylons, amber, fur wraps.
Wartime Films (English): *Rebecca, Mrs Miniver, Brief Encounter.*
Wartime Films (French): *Odette.*
Wartime Colours: earth tones.
Wartime Hats: perched beaky wool hats tipped over the face, trilbies.
Forties People: Greer Garson, Joan Greenwood (that voice), Bette Davis, Judy Garland singing to the troops.
Forties Designer Star: Hardy Amies.
Forties Places: somewhere in Surrey, blitzed London, Paris under occupation.
Forties Photographer: Norman Parkinson, Brassaï.
Forties Sportstyle: golf (particularly for the co-respondent shoes).

O YES VERY FIFTIES

Of all the decades the modern designer is in love with, the fifties it will always be with passion. Here beginneth the absolute reign of the fashion photographer and the fashion magazine, serious make-up and the big graphic hat. The fifties style from the New Look to the Capri Pant was just made for the catwalk and café pose. It just *has* to be looked at.

The fifties look is for the witty girl who loves to accessorize: rocks, hats, handbags, long gloves with little black dresses. The fifties look is for the supermarket American who loves to dance in print frocks and socks, her hair tied in a ponytail or a broad headband.

The fifties look is for the bohemian girl who likes striped tops, stovepipes and shades and all the gamine chic. Show me a girl who doesn't adore the fifties and I will show you a liar.

Fifties Movies: *Dance with a Stranger, Funny Face, La Dolce Vita, Absolute Beginners, Summer Holiday.*
Fifties Places: Left Bank, coffee bars, New York.
Fifties Designer Star: Givenchy.
Fifties Photographers: Penn, Avedon.

Fifties Colour: the fifties saw the birth of black, beatnik black, cocktail black. It loved the camera.
Fifties Details: the compact, eyebrows, high hair, cars.
Fifties People: jazz musicians and existentialists.
Fifties Heroes: Elvis, Jack Kerouac, Audrey Hepburn.

FIFTIES FEMMES FATALES

Top, *Lauren Bacall with bubble car*
Above, *Audrey Hepburn with cigarette holder*
Right, *At the Coffee Bar: Black and white striped cha-cha shirt and head band by Rifat Ozbek with a cool straw by Graham Smith*
Opposite, *At the Cocktail Bar: Coveri's blue and silver cocktail frock with key accessories; black evening gloves, beads and spex*

THE FAB
SIXTIES

There are two looks for the sixties: one has got to do with vinyl, the other one with paisley, but both had their origins in Swinging London. If the fifties treated modern girl like a star, the sixties turned her into a doll. A skinny space doll with huge eyes and a hunger for a good time. This is the age for the mini (skirt and car), the age of the long boot and the crazy dayglo fabrics. The paisley version grows the doll's hair (even irons it straight), gives it sandals for its feet and flowers for its hair.

Modern Girl, not being a victim, takes the kitsch humour of both looks and mixes them together, i.e. a psychedelic velvet mini dress with pale make-up. She would never go as far as to wear anything resembling a kaftan.

Fab Designers (then): Betsy Johnson, Mary Quant, Courrèges, Ossie Clark.
Fab Designers (now): Stephen Sprouse, Scott Crolla.
Fab Details: popsocks, hipster belts, body paint, beads, bare feet.
Fab Films: *Blow Up*, *Sweet Charity*, *Taste of Honey*, *Georgy Girl*.
Fab People: Sandie Shaw, Edie

Sedgewick, Dusty Springfield. The sixties saw the birth of model as superstar – Penelope Tree, Twiggy, Jean Shrimpton.
Fab Places: The Factory, Chelsea, Woodstock, India.
Fab Fabrix: chainmail, PVC, denim, crushed velvet.
Fab Hair: The Vidal Sassoon cut, Afro, big hair.

SWING OUT SISTERS
Opposite, *Chelsea Girl by Courrèges*
Sixties Models: Jean Shrimpton (top) and *Penelope Tree* (above)
Left, *Into the Groove: hot pink silk jersey mini with cut-out peace sign, pink satin shorts and sparkly Lycra tights; right, satin jacket and drainpipes – all by Stephen Sprouse*

MEN'S DRESSING

en's dressing, cross dressing, is not about looking like a man. Men's dressing is about borrowing the best looks from the boys, stealing their tailoring, their shirts, their formality and their favourite hat and making it look even better. Men's dressing is the worst plagiarist in the wardrobe.

Modern Girl begins at the top with the trilby, worn at a jaunty angle, or a homburg or panama or a beret, just so long as they always look ironic and not like Daddy. However, she does borrow his haircut (even his barber), his watch and his cufflinks, especially those silken coloured knots, but she doesn't really go for his ties. She might just tie a cravat, or borrow the way he has his scarf, casually about his neck. Most of all she grabs his formal wear, the big coat, the suit and the severe shirting, the dinner trousers and the shoes. The best thing about Daddy was the way he had essential wardrobe figured out – the way there was always one outfit for one occasion, all the shirts neatly folded in one drawer and his shoes immaculately polished. She loves all the accessories from the hipflask to the umbrella, all classic, all timeless. No, she doesn't want to be like Daddy but she sure likes his style.

The Shirt: the big stiff collared white, the button down, the wing and the Eton collar, the blue and white stripe, the Fred Perry.

The Formal: the tuxedo, the mess jacket, the tailcoat, the waistcoat, the cravat, the tie pin (see Alternative Tux, Party!).

The Shoe: the brogue, the penny loafer, the co-respondent, the short sock.

The Coat: the double-breasted overcoat, the tweed, the trench (see Classic Coats), the car coat, the velvet collar, the deep pockets.

WELL SUITED

Above, *Gender Bender: Annie Lennox*
Below, *Ralph Lauren's country squire: black velvet suit, purple wool waistcoat, cream lace jabot and cuffs*
Below right, *Master of Ceremonies: tartan trousers from Sarah Windsor and tail coat from Hacketts*
Opposite, *Mastering the Theme: Matisse's black cashmere short coat worn with black pullover and gaberdine trousers by Romeo Gigli*

MUDLARK

Mudlark style is gamine at its most boyish. It's the Victorian waif meets the post-nuclear schoolboy.

It's the bakerboy hat of the sixties, it's the proud cockney sparrows designed by John Galliano. Mudlark style is a patched and pocketed, oversized and undersized with the wrong buttons done up. It's clever and insolent with tailoring that cocks a snoot at the establishment. It favours collarless white or striped shirts with baggy trousers held up with braces, waistcoats, jerkins or sleeveless jersey, caps, belts and pocketful of keys and coins. This Edwardian ragamuffin wears shoes that she can run away in – men's brogues and lace-ups (from second-hand stores) or buttoned boots. Always carries a silk handkerchief.

MUDLARKING ABOUT

Above, *Tomboy-tough woollens and tweed caps*
Opposite, *Rumpled wool jacket, striped silk moiré halterneck, striped cotton shirt and brocade waistcoat – all by John Galliano*

UNIFORM

Uniform dressing is a sharp-eyed regimented style that takes its influences from global institutions that range from the Brownies cap to the bellhop's cap. It is not to be confused with dressing up, draws the line at camouflage and never loses its sense of humour.

Some uniforms are better suited to modern style than others. There is nothing witty about appearing as a Vietnam grunt but a scarlet coat cut *à la* Waterloo plus boots never fails. The trick is to find the romance of uniform, a mixture of utility (flying jackets) and dress (braided band jackets).

MECHANIC

Mechanic style is a working style that doesn't give a damn about getting its hands dirty. It loves the romance of the trainyards, the toolsheds, the docklands. It rides a bike when it can.

Mechanic style collects tough blue overalls and dungarees, wears them with white T-shirts or large coloured shirts, biker's leathers and boots. It mixes the rough with the smooth, lace with the dungarees, flirtskirt with the leathers. This tough girl likes to keep the issue confused and never wants to look like the janitor.

REGULATION DRILL
Above, *Marlene Dietrich, 1944*
Below, *Black and red stripe woollen spenser and trousers by Liette with a beret by Fraizzoli*
Below right, *Striped linen sweater and silk skirt by Calvin Klein*
Opposite, *Silk brocade side-buttoned stove pipes by Genny, wool zipped blouson by Reporter*

ARMY SURPLUS CLASSICS

WW2 leather and sheepskin flying helmets, white singlets, heavy laced boots, canvas belts, chinos, waiters' cropped tuxes, chefs' white jackets and blue and white checked trousers, regimental trousers with stripes, blue overalls, navy reefer jackets.

BACK TO SCHOOL

Schoolgirl dressing is the Lolita of the wardrobe, no one can resist her shortskirt charms. The essence of school dressing is a mixture of the anarchic and the demure, the St Trinian's meets the Prime of Miss Jean Brodie. The demure is the long dark gymslip with prim collared white blouse, plain stocking and sensible shoes. This student is grave and sweet and likes a coat with a princess line in plain wool, a panama hat and a long woollen scarf. She carries her books in a satchel and reads them on the bus with a puritan concentration and a pair of tortoiseshell granny specs.

Her anarchic sister don't like to read. She wears blazers with the sleeves rolled up and schoolbadges that she shouldn't all upside down. Her flirtskirts are short and pleated, kilts and Just William long shorts. When she plays rough she wears flannel culottes and a collared games jersey. She loves over-the-knee socks for that gamine *école* look.

School Colours: grey, navy, olive, plum, mustard.
School Hair: plaits, ponytails, Eton crop.
School Coat: that mac (see Classic Coats).
School Details: stripes, mottoes, the white shirt, lunchboxes, freckles, tie pins, charm bracelets.

COLLEGE

This is the clean cut graduate look that plays hookey on fine afternoons. It mixes tweed and plaid with large collared shirts in sweet American style. It wears a cap at a schoolboy angle, it might even wear a pair of knickerbockers. One thing is for sure, it never ties a tie or wraps a scarf like the regulations say it should.

NAVAL PARADE

Of all the military uniforms, none is so dashing as navy- the colour and the concept. Think of those Soviet sailor jackets, those *Cruel Sea* duffles, all that 18th-century midshipman rig! Retro girl loves a sailor, whatever his rank: she wears a cropped ensign's jacket with baggy whites and marine stripes, she wears a tailored officer's jacket shining with brass buttons and a crisp white shirt. She adores a sailor collar on any occasion (as long as it is not on a sugary drop waisted dress).

Navy Films: *Battleship Potemkin, Mutiny on the Bounty.*
Navy Details: cream breeches, whistles, peaked caps, tailcoats.
Sailorcollar Designer Star: John Galliano.

SUMMER AND WINTER REPORT

Above, *Cream cricket linens from Workers for Freedom, thick white cotton cardigan from Edina Ronay and flannel cap from Kent and Curwen* Below, *Harris tweed with velveteen collar and lurex flecked pockets by Vivienne Westwood*

GIRLS' SCHOOL

Opposite, *Suit of worsted wool with zipped bustier waistcoat by Joe Casely Hayford*

160

FASHION DETAILS

Fashion without detail is like mutton without caper sauce, perfectly fine and dandy but O so much more delicious with. What would Modern Girl do without her box of accessories, her little surprises from the wardrobe, the sudden unexpected ironic twist of pearl, her favourite hat, that bag she bought so long ago in Venice, or was it Rome?

The fashion detail, whether hat, glove or shoe, has the power to alter radically the same frock, fifteen ways or more. Whether you tie a chain or a thick leather belt, put on black opaque tights or sheer, wear a wig, pile on costume jewellery or simply don a pair of gauntlets, the look can always be changed. The fashion detail is the chameleon effect.

Fashion details divide between the classic and the contemporary. Classic details are such as the wide tan belt and the panama hat, which appear every year, though in a different spirit. Contemporary details move with each season so that a plain leather belt could find itself wrapped twice about the hips or waspily round the waist; a scarf round the neck, on the head, gently draping or stuffed in a pocket. Fashion details cover every part of the image from the way you cut your hair to the way you swing your handbag (or satchel or suitcase).

So start at the top and work your way down. It always pays to pay attention.

GRAPHIC DETAILS
Black and white dressing with bangle by Pellini, gloves by Alpo, shoes by Fausto Santini and handbag by Nino Candido

162

HATBOX

Hatgirl is into statements. She can't resist walking into a place and making heads turn. Hatgirl wouldn't have been any big deal in the days when everyone wore hats, but now they don't, she is (or fondly imagines so). The trick about the hat is not to let it wear you. The hat has got to look as though it's a natural extension of you and your outfit. You are not trying to win a prize at Ascot, you are being amusing and chic (you could even be trying alternatively to keep your head cool or warm).

Hatgirl has a hat for every occasion and collects hatboxes with a vengeance.

COCKTAIL HAT

The point of the Cocktail Hat is *wit*. It is born at an advantage, being small and precariously perched, but the true Cocktail Hat is shrieking something as well. Look, I'm wild with pink feathers! Look, I'm pretending to be a vase of flowers! Talk to me! The Cocktail Hat wants to be in *Breakfast at Tiffany's*. Not for the fainthearted.

STRAW HAT

The hat fabric of summer. Taken as twenties cloche (see Retro), Edwardian big hat with roses and veils (see Retro), country bashed straw, hippy floppy straw, wide-brim straw with frayed edges (worn with cotton or muslin bob cap underneath for the Deep South look), smart coloured urban straw and the panama.

WOOL HAT

Definitely for keeping warm, the Wool Hat is not a great show-off. Tightfitting beanies in navy or black worn elfin style. The only Wool Hat that is allowed a bobble is a tam o'shanter. For balaclava and other wintersport directions see Snow, Action!

MEN'S HATS

Men have great classics while women have the party frocks. Modern girl scorns the wedding hat as an art form, and borrows most of her hatstyle from the men. The best shapes being: the beret (see Boulevard Chic, Another Country), the trilby, the bowler, the topper and the fedora. She wouldn't be seen dead in anything approximating a cricket boater.

THE PILLBOX

Hatgirl knows only Jackie O looked great in this.

CAPS

The cap is hatgirl in *très* gamine mode. Bakerboy, fisherboy, Chinese boy, cabin boy. This peak is worn with irreverence.

STRUCTURAL HATS

This is the modern hat that likes a good graphic shape (naturally it's

THE STRAW HAT
Opposite, *Black sailor hat by Patricia Underwood*
Top, *Huge picture hat by Graham Smith*
Above, *Black-bowed hat by Bernstock-Speirs*

165

CROWNING GLORIES

Right, *A tall, black Cossack hat by Hermes* Inset, *Navy stove-pipe straw with shot silk taffetta by Lisa Miller* Opposite top, *White straw from Valentino* Opposite below left, *Black wool beret from Kangol pinned with a gold, silver, diamond and mother-of-pearl menagerie* Opposite below right, *Swakura fur cap by Stephen Jones*

in black). It's usually also in a fabric that will stand up looking dramatic rather than stagey, a cossack hat rather than a bearskin hat. This hat likes being worn indoors and get *furious* if anybody else tries it on.

ETHNIC HATS
Astrakhan to matador (see Another Country).

DECORATION
Very occasionally flowers. Sometimes feathers (see Shooting, Action!) sometimes a contrasting scarf wrapped about the edge. If the hat comes plain, hatgirl usually leaves it well alone.

ARTIST'S BERET
If you want to look like Rembrandt you can wear a very large beret in black velvet. You could also look like a sweet Victorian child. Hatgirl don't want to look like either.

Hat Hates: anything suburban granny (i.e. a viscose turban), anything in real fur, hats worn on the back of the head.

Hat Heroes: modern girl is spoilt for British designers. Her faves include Stephen Jones, Fred Bare, Andrew Wilkie and Philip Somerville (for cocktail).

168

HAIR

Ever since Iron Age girl first grabbed those scissors, what you do with your hair determines your visual self more than any other raiment. Hair declares what group you belong to, which race, sex, class and creed. It also expresses your acquiescence or revolt against such groupings, historically shown by the bobbing of hair in the twenties, the 'feminist frizz' of the seventies, the defiant growing of hair by the outsider bikers and hippies, the militaristic short-back-and-sides and the nihilistic Mohican cut. Personally, Modern Girl can't decide whether she is roundhead or cavalier, she does a hair rethink practically every month.

SHORT HAIR

The boyish cut of the Eighties is sleek and sculpted with gels (think Lee Miller), very short and feathered (think Mia Farrow in the sixties), or gamine and tousled. It is kept in trim as often as possible, at the new wave barbers such as Atlas.

THE POWER BOB

The exec cut, the cut that hires and fires, this bob is a remote relation of the funtime Twenties bob. This bob has not one strand out of place, the hair swings like a knife through the air but keeps the wearer looking sweet. The revenge of clever women.

HAIR UP

Up hair is not a hair do, it is not Mari Wilson with a beehive or five hours in the hairdresser's. Up hair is neither a fussy bun showoff nor a prim schoolmistress's knot at the nape. Up hair is coolly executed: a French pleat or classic chignon, sometimes adorned with silk ribbons and rosettes. Up hair is also the dance ponytail with black velvet ribbon and very cropped fringe (very Gigi).

HEADGIRLS
Opposite, *Shaping up with hair rolled and wrapped with satin ribbon by Didier Malige for Jean Louis David*
Top Knots: Black stretch velvet turban with feathers (top) and
Headgirl by Kerry Warn
(above)

THE LONG AND SHORT OF IT: *Fringe Benefits by Christian* (above left); *Slick pony-tail caught by a black velvet bow* (above right); *Long, sleek bob by Kerry Warn* (below); *New Waves by Christopher Brooker for Vidal Sassoon* (opposite)

LONG HAIR

Out of vogue in the hard asexual years, long hair returned to modern style with the advent of the Empire Girl designed by John Galliano and Romeo Gigli. Soft, straight and romantic, this long hair had a gentle fringe and is sometimes worn in a loose plait. Its flamboyant cousin is big hair, the long hair with volume and no restraint. Long hair is never permed. Though a certain amount of play with multiple top knots and Regency ringlets went on in the fashion pages, Modern Girl could never take a fake curl too seriously.

TINT HINT

Hair colour is a fickle child that changes its mind each season: once peroxide blonde (short), then Titian red (long), now raven black (long and Hispanic). Thanks to science you can keep with the hip hue. But keep the highlights in trim, nothing looks more depressing than rootshow. And only punks and French schoolchildren have green hair.

SPEX

Although there has been a fashion detail leaning towards clear-glass wear (Lois Lane batwings in France, granny wire rims in the UK), by spex generally we mean shades. The ultimate expression of cool. And when we say shades we are not talking beachwear or holiday frames to hide the glare, we are talking straight urban street and restaurant style. Glamour glass.

Spex are *never* sunglasses, they would never have a designer label (such as Pierre Cardin, Porsche). Spex are for keeping yourself mysterious, particularly at night or after a night. As in the shirt collar, there are subtle shifts of mood each year (a lean away from goggles, a veering towards the wraparound), but there are just two rules before you take the season's decision:

1. Make sure they're impenetrable; you don't want anyone to see your eyes. Black, dense brown, dark green, dark pink or mirrored (except for the wraparound which makes anyone look like a second-rate ski instructor).

2. Make sure they are mean. Nice, friendly frames are no good. Spex are for chilling out society (see James Dean). Even if you are wearing sensible colours, like the man who wears an immaculate suit with designer stubble, the spex will give you that instant nuance of being on the wrong side, that existential frisson, that rebel chic.

Spexfax

Spex look good anywhere, anytime, except if you are trying to have a conversation, when that fashion detail just gets in the way (unless you are trying to undermine that conversation in which case spex are *perfect*).

Spex do not look terrific with ballgowns or Edwardian blouses (unless you wear them in a spirit of riotous irony).

Spex do look terrific with suits, swimsuits, little black dresses, little else or anything continental.

Spex do not have long, plastic chains attached to them (clear spex might have a black cord like those of a Chandler secretary).

Spex do not have a plastic pouch to hide in when not in use, or something charming in appliqué. They like to live in leather (old or new) or one of those hard cases that snap shut very fiercely. Or your top pocket.

Spex have no fans in bosses, parents or policemen. If you don't want to antagonize authority, I suggest you take them *off*.

No. 1: first pair of shades made in 1885 in Philadelphia.
Most Copied: *those* Ray-Bans.
Spex Movie Models: Marcello Mastroianni in *La Dolce Vita* (Wayfarers). Audrey Hepburn in *Breakfast at Tiffany's* (lollipops). Sue Lyon in *Lolita*. The killers in *The Killers*.
Wraparound Hero: Peter Fonda in *Easy Rider*.
Wraparound Heroine: Jackie O at the White House.
Hideaway Models: Garbo, Jean-Luc Godard, Roy Orbison.

CLASSIC COOL
Opposite, *Silver-mirrored spex*
This page, *Black half-rim clear glass*
Top, *The tortoiseshell Ray-Ban*
Above, *Sunscreens by Xun for Private Eyes*

173

SCARF

The modern scarf is the prankster of the essential wardrobe, the cat amongst the pigeons. It can tie around the hair, around the head, go under a hat, over a hat, out of a pocket, pretend to be a cummerbund or a stock or simply be draped and knitted round the neck in several witty ways. It can be the sudden spot of colour amongst all that black, the sheer contradictory clash, the unexpected pattern against plain. Modern Girl has collected scarves for years from paisley shawls to mock Hermès. An Indian scarf even doubles as a clever cloth shoulder bag on the beach.

THE MUFFLER

The warm woollen, the comforter of winter, this scarf should never be mean or artificial (try lambswool or cashmere). It should never look as if granny just knitted it with long straggly tassels (although a crochet shawl worn with a big coat is OK). Pale colours are best: vanilla, milk grey or total black. The college scarf is not cool at college and certainly isn't out of college.

THE CHIFFON SCARF

The wisp of teatime delicacy, worn quietly draped with muted dressing. **Chiffon colours:** pale violet, rose, lemon and ivory, floral patterned or plain, or sorbet brights for creative clash. **Chiffon heroine:** Georgina von Etsdorf.

COWBOY COTTON

The rugged patterned work scarf worn in a twist with open-necked shirt and denim – or on the head, as immortalized by Bruce Weber.

MIX AND MATCH
Below, *Paisley print handkerchief square*
Below left, *Antique lilac and cream chiffon scarf*
Opposite, *Royal blue lambswool muffler by Mondi*

GLOVES

Once upon a time all the nice girls wore a pair of gloves. Or carried them at least. Or made sure the servants wore them at mealtimes. Gloves were, and are, a sign of distance from the hurly burly of the real world. I may have to shake your hand/eat at your table/pat your child's head but I don't have to feel it, I don't have to mean it. Gloves are a sycophant's best friend.

Not all gloves, of course, are quite so arrogant. Take the humble pair of woollens. Now, Modern Girl, egalitarian at all times, never baulks at a creamy pair of lambswools once the frost has hit the park. In fact she positively buys three new pairs each winter. Black, navy and the aforesaid vanilla. Nothing folksy or patterned (she likes to look her age), certainly nothing that hangs on strings round her neck as though Nanny were making sure. Definitely no mittens, except if they are in sheepskin (see Snow, Action!).

Winter is glovegirl's best friend. She can't wait to spend that little bit extra on a pair of skinny leather (calf, kid or pigskin). So *classique!* (She dreams of the glove shops on the Ponte Vecchio, simply every colour and so cheap!) She loves them skintight and unlined, she loves them slightly chunky and lined in fur. When she feels particularly fierce and bad, she covets pairs of gauntlets – without studs. It is fine to look as though you keep hawks, another thing to look like a bit part from *Mad Max IV*.

One thing is for sure, in spite of total accessory love, glovegirl would never go *one inch* with anyone who drove in motorist gloves.

And when it comes to evening and glamour dressing, nothing can keep her from the dressing-up box. Bare arms are just an excuse for long, long satin and silk. Cream, black, crimson, yellow, aquamarine. As long as it keeps plain – just one plain stone ring for show-offs.

It has to be said that glovegirl is no sportsfan. Nevertheless she is fanatical about sportsgloves. She just loves to watch those big gloves in action, baseball pitchers to cricket wicketkeepers. And she energetically collects fingerless leather cyclists' or yachting gloves and riding gloves, the string and leather variety (see Action!). She mourns the summer: white cotton or lace gloves are OK but a bit demure for glovegirl who is a wicked girl at heart (and will throw down the gauntlet at *any* provocation).

Glove Hero: Robert Browning who always wore yellow kid.

Glove Anti-hero: Michael Jackson who only wears one white cotton.

Glovelove: the fifties, the Renaissance, old-fashioned department stores that keep their gloves in drawers, wooden glove bowls in hallways, lavender and tan.

HAND IN GLOVE
Top, *Taking up the gauntlet with Azzedine Alaia*
Above, *Frogged long black suede gloves with crimson satin cuffs by Valentino*
Opposite, *Black leather gloves by Dents with a wristful of Chanel chains*

COSTUME JEWELLERY

Once upon a time it was only right and proper to flaunt jewels, if you had them. The concept of wearing fake gems, of pretending a life-style without lands, was unthinkable. Now the piling on of paste is wildly indiscriminate. Anyone can be an heiress (even the real one would leave genuine stones in the vault). Modern Girl loves costume jewellery. Her casket overflows.

ETHNIC
Deep colour beads, silver bangles, gold filigree, plain African rings, elaborate Indian necklaces. From Mexico to Tibet, Modern Girl seeks out the intricate workmanship and the primitive inspiration. She is a *nouvelle* hippy and loves to mix modern urban clothes with ethnic details.

OLD GOLD
Restrained jewellery for careful nostalgic dressing. Edwardian sweet brooches and drop earrings. Silver sown with tiny stones, plain gold rings, hearts and roses, charm bracelets.

ANCIENT GOLD
Inspired by the archaeological dig, this style takes the shape of animals, shells and symbols (cf Greece and Egypt). Gold and verdigris (often looks as if it has been rescued from the sea). Best worn in summer with plain earth colours. **Designers:** Jennifer Corker, Wright & Teague.

ETHNIC STYLE
Above, *Big, bold bangles in silver, natural and stained wood by Dinny Hall*
Opposite, *Beaded coral, amber, tortoiseshell and silver by Paulo Scarta, Gigli at Callaghan and Donnatella Pellini*

CHANEL CHAIN-GANG

Extravagant wearing of gold chains and pearls, bangles at wrists and knuckleduster baroque rings.

DIAMANTÉ

The flash false diamond, the vulgar stone for the party girl who doesn't give a damn. She also loves the fake ruby, emerald and sapphire but diamanté is best and best when it's big. **Bauble designers:** Butler and Wilson, Monty Don. **Treasure Chest Hero:** Eric Beamon.

SCULPTURAL SILVER

Designer streamline, the black of the jewellery box. Asymmetric, abstract and very modern, sculptural silver only wants stark clothes so it can show off. Silver hero: Tom Binns.

NO NO NANETTE

Leather thongs, thin gold chains, pearl chokers (and all Sloane clichés), gold studs, ankle chains, belly chains, crucifixes (unless large and ironic and by Jean Paul Gaultier).
Beyond costume: Tiaras, nose jewellery, safety pins (*passé* punk).
Badge note: If you've got something to say, *say* it.
Watch note: Hip ticks are old boys with plain parchment faces and brown leather straps, silver cocktail watches from the forties, fake Rolexes or cheap dimestores faces worn over sleeves (preferably more than one). The Swatch may be a success financially but . . .

Opposite top, *Old Times . . . New Times from Omega, Tissot and Raymond Weil*
Opposite below, *Wear Your Face on Your Sleeve:* right, *Modern watch by Supre,* left, *Antique Minerva from Aaron Fabei*
Opposite, main picture, *Sculptural Models: Aluminium alloy cuffs and earrings by David Millman*
Left, *A chainstore of gilt, pearl and a dash of diamante by Chanel*

BAGS OF STYLE
Right, *Round black patent shoulderbag by Prada*
Below left, *Large brown leather sac, with a Louis Vuitton handbag*
Below right, *Brown crocodile by Chanel*

THE HANDBAG

Now, it has to be said that the decline in formality is almost entirely due to the disappearance of the handbag as an essential commodity. The handbag, the two or one short-handled, leather bound, snap-shut handbag, is no longer a priority in the world of accessory. It might be another kind of bag, a satchel, say, or a briefcase, but it won't be a handbag. The traditional handbag is dead, even for the most ironic dresser. Modern Girl just has other things to do with her hands (besides, where would she fit the Filofax?). She might have a small bag, quilted *à la* Chanel, but you can bet your last sovereign that it will be on long thin handles, that she will wear it slung across her shoulder like a bullet holder and that somewhere lurks a large basket or holdall with the rest of her life inside.

Modern Girl just cannot approach life with one stick of lipstick and a doorkey. She moves from work to play and travels too much to be without her essential kit. So somewhere in the late sixties, when control meant living as an urban nomad, Modern Girl threw in that patent, white plastic or whatyouwill bag and took herself a serious sac.

SERIOUS SAC 1: THE BRIEFCASE

The Briefcase is a real workcase. It knows nothing about play. Briefcase loves schedules and breakfast meetings and never leaves its Am-Ex behind. In the seventies, when the serious sac tried to show off its goodsport image, the Briefcase took many forms: it could be a music case or a baby leather suitcase or a croc Gladstone bag, it could be primary coloured plastic, see-through plastic, wire-meshed metal or a Mickey Mouse lunchbox. It could even be your old school satchel, Daddy's old briefcase, a leftover portfolio or violin case, just as long as it didn't look like the real thing.

In the eighties, when being serious, especially about work, was *in*, the Briefcase stopped pretending and putting on silly hats. It started to be itself.

(But never in grey Samsonite.)

SERIOUS SAC 2: THE RUCKSACK

The Rucksack is the bag for the urban adventurer. In the mid-eighties the Rucksack shed its Youth Club bri-nylon image and became the bag of hip. First spotted in stripes on the Italian *pistes*, where it was *de rigueur* for the *Benetoni alpini*, it was soon designed in tan leather, black Japanese nylon, even in thick ethnic cloth. It was the bag worn to work and to the nightclub. Its two crossover straps looked terrific with black clothes and Doc Martens, even though it did take at least ten minutes to take off, undo and replace as before when shopping.

The more sportif took in later months to the New York bike bag, like a newspaper bag in tough nylon with one broad crossover strap (the real thing, especially the *Guardian* newspaper bag, in fluorescent orange, enjoyed street cred for a whole summer).

The rural equivalent of this was the wickerwork creel with canvas strap (see Fishing, Action!) or the seafaring duffle bag but these never impressed the doorman.

BAG THAT
Above, *Brown leather and
crocodile knapsack*
Right, *Chaingang by Chanel*
Opposite page, *The timeless
travel trunk*

SERIOUS SAC 3: THE SMALL BAG

The Small Bag is for those who really can't turn up at lunch swinging a sac the size of a picnic basket. The picnic basket is there but it is left at the office and the Small Bag is there with the essentials only (the chequebook, not the provisions).

The Small Bag has to be leather and it has to be small (no mumsy medium sizes). It can be open (the bucket), zipped, round, square or oval but it has to be classic and has to have that strap (or chain).

The cousin to the Small Bag is the Evening Bag, that slip of black beaded silk, that show-off in gold and tapestry, but Modern Girl leaves it well alone. She doesn't like to have a good time with the equivalent of an expensive packet of crisps under her arm or in her hand (Modern Girl is a fan of hatcheck).

SERIOUS SAC 4: THE ETHNIC BAG

The Ethnic Bag is the bag of summer and its great statement is the Moroccan basket. The Moroccan basket is a subtly coloured woven sac with two straw or leather handles. It is in no way to be confused with the shopping basket. The Moroccan basket is made for the beach and can still be hooked on to the shoulders (key point). The Moroccan basket doesn't actually have to come from Morocco. It can come from Greece, it can come from Peru, just as long as it's from abroad and isn't in plastic.

The Ethnic Bag alternative is a piece of Indian cotton knotted at both ends and worn like a saddle bag.

LUGGAGE NOTE

In the golden days of travel, luggage was as vital as the clothes that were packed in it (perfectly ironed in between pieces of tissue paper). The sea trunk with banded wooden hoops was the symbol of a grand trip. Now voyager who carries her own and resents paying overweight at airports takes a large soft bag in canvas or Japanese black nylon. She is quite tempted by the idea of the leather suitcase in markets but, being a realist, resists. The only hard case she allows is the navy or grey Globetrotter which is tough enough for any journey (and can be sat upon).

Sometimes she toys, in a retro mood, with the return to the vanity case. But only toys.

Bagstyle Point: no one ever carried anything alluring in a tote bag.

FOOTNOTES

For a long time fashion shoes were simple. There was one boot for winter, there was that kind of heel for that year. But now there is confusion in the shoe cupboard. There are flat shoes and high heels, pointed toes and chisel toes, frivolous retro shoes and serious modern shoes and the thigh boot is no longer something to view with derision. What does Modern Girl do? She knows exactly when to wear what, knows that though a pair of plimsolls can look witty with a strict designer suit, a pair of Doc Martens with the New Cocktail Frock only looks ridiculous.

Modern Girl knows her essential wardrobe and draws a fine list of essential shoes:

PUMPS

Flat ballet pumps in black (essential beatnik footwear). Black patent with matt bow for the Alternative Tuxedo in dancing mood. Both available from dance shops (the Scottish dancing shoe with long cross-over laces looks fine but the sole is too soft for outerwear). Do not wear real pink ballet pumps with satin ribbons.

JAZZ SHOE

Another dance shoe but laced. Good in white for summer lace-up, or black suede. Can make feet look midget.

BAR SHOE

Not to be confused with the Start-rite school shoe. The Bar Shoe has a sculptured heel and loves pale colours (see Twenties, Retro). Dance equivalent: the character, flamenco or tap shoe, in black or scarlet.

THE LACE-UP

The Lace-up is the strong flat that strides out in all weathers and is not afraid of walking. The aristo Lace-up is the brogue with the famous holed leather originally for letting bog water seep through (although it has to be said that Modern Girl prefers the pavements for these). The Lace-up likes black and tan leather and suede. Its sports version is the co-respondent gold shoe with fringe, without spikes, its tough urban version is ...

DOC MARTEN

Doc Marten, brat of the boulevard and the favourite sole of the bovver. It symbolizes all that is tough and aggressive and modern and has given endless street cred to many a fashion victim. The Doc Marten is the 501 of the shoe cupboard and Modern Girl takes it in its original black. She also wears it with black and knows that it can make her feet look *enormous* (she doesn't care).

PIXIE SHOE

The flat shoe with a point for the Quixotic reveller. The Pixie shoe is taken from medieval romance and its elfin shape has been celebrated in diverse corners from the white plastic Chelsea Boot by Mary Quant to the oyster satin court shoe by Emma Hope. Fey and utterly charming, this is no shoe for realists.

FOOTNOTES
Above, *Silver-buckled black patent flattie*
Below, *Rose-sprigged tapestry pumps by Johnny Moke*
Opposite, *Black and white canvas high heels by Chanel*

SLIPPER

Related in spirit to both the Pixie and the Pump, the Slipper is a minimal shoe that goes with virtually every kind of dressing, especially in elastic-gathered suede. The Slipper for evening in satin or velvet can go to extravagant colours – violet, emerald and gold – and often plays with monograms (fake, of course).

PATENT

The notion of patent has bad childhood memories of the party shoe one never wanted to wear. Patent does slip in and out of fashion. Best for pointed lace-ups and pumps and always in black.

SHOE BAGS

So chic, so useful. A must.

HEELS

For years fashion would not be seen in anything that went higher than two centimetres. In a world dominated by leggings and the Japanese, there was no place for them. And then came the return of the serious short skirt which just died for a pair of serious high heels. And now, no matter how sternly principled, essential ward-robe has to have one pair of high and one pair of medium severely tailored courts in black suede or leather with a pointed toe (almost, indeed, a stiletto).

PLIMSOLL

See Track, Action!, and also for baseball boots.

SANDALS

A collection of ethnic sandals: woven Indian etc. Always for summer. No flip flops.

SLINGBACKS

Katherine Hamnett brought back the Slingback with her spiderwoman spikes. The only others to have are the evening pale satin heels, preferably by Maud Frizon.

BOOTS

The ankle boot, worn toughly laced (related to the Doc Marten) or in honey sheepskin, zipped granny style. The riding boots (see Hunting, Action!). The very tall, over the knee, over the top boot for show-offs in black leather or suede. The wellington boot for mud and wet (never with a heel, always long).

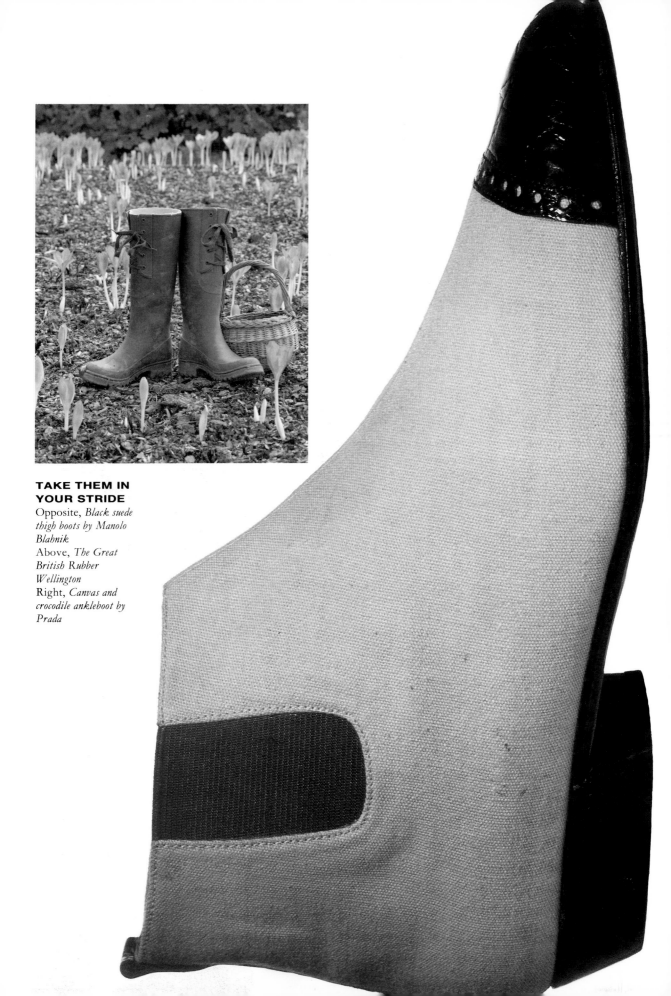

TAKE THEM IN YOUR STRIDE

Opposite, *Black suede thigh boots by Manolo Blahnik*
Above, *The Great British Rubber Wellington*
Right, *Canvas and crocodile ankleboot by Prada*

PHOTOGRAPHIC CREDITS